SEW SERENDIPITY
SEWING WORKBOOK

Tips, Tricks and Projects for Those Who Love Sewing

Kay Whitt

SEW SERENDIPITY
SEWING WORKBOOK

*Tips, Tricks and Projects for
Those Who Love Sewing*

Kay Whitt

KRAUSE PUBLICATIONS
Cincinnati, Ohio

Table of Contents

INTRODUCTION

Welcome to *Sew Serendipity Sewing Workbook*. The format of this book is a little different from *Sew Serendipity* and *Sew Serendipity Bags*. Rather than create another purely project-driven book for my readers, I wanted to write a book that would answer some of the questions I get asked most often as a designer. As such, *Sew Serendipity Sewing Workbook* is packed with informative sewing advice articles, providing you with helpful insights, tips and tricks of the trade. There is even some space for you to record your thoughts as you go and contemplate your sewing goals, much like a sewing journal. I want you to think of this book as a means of recording your journey through sewing, with time to reflect on what you have learned and how it will impact your sewing in the future.

All of the information found in the sewing advice articles comes from my own experiences throughout my many years of sewing and designing. I hope that you will find this to be a great instructional companion to your sewing, that you learn a few new skills here and there, and that you will come back to refer to the valuable information I have put together for you.

Obviously, this book just wouldn't be complete without the addition of a few projects! Scattered throughout are easy-to-sew projects perfect for applying and practicing the tips and techniques discussed in the sewing advice articles. I've included two such projects for each season—spring, summer, fall and winter—giving you something to work on all year round. So, without further ado, let's get started!

Setting up Your Studio

We all dream about having a huge amount of space to work in, right? Unfortunately, we all have to live within our own respective realities, so we have to be creative with what we have. I know a lot of people squeeze in their sewing spaces wherever they can. I used a spare bedroom for many years before actually deciding to chuck the bed and get a real workspace going, and I do this stuff for a living! I can't tell you what a difference it made, and I wouldn't trade it for the world!

If you can dedicate a space exclusively for your sewing, it will make your life easier, even if that space is only a corner of a room. If at all possible, it is best to avoid using a staple piece of furniture in your home—like a dining room table, for example—as your workspace. It is a hassle to move all of your supplies and projects-in-progress in order to free up space to eat dinner, and that always seems to be just about the time you are really rolling on a project! By dedicating a space to your work, you can walk away from it and not disturb your progress. I believe this is one of the ways that you can be more productive with your sewing. When you have to pack up all the time, it can leave not only your project in disarray, but your thoughts about it as well.

That being said, it is also important to have a nice assortment of sewing tools at your disposal. For the most part, sewing supplies are rather inexpensive and can make a huge difference to how quickly you can accomplish any particular task. The following list details some of the most important tools that you need for a productive sewing space.

- - - - - - - MEASURING TOOLS - - - - - -

Dressmaker's Measuring Tape: This tape is about 60" long and is very flexible. It's perfect for taking body measurements and other varied measuring uses when you need a flexible tool.

Dressmaker's Adjustable Ruler: This is a 6"-long ruler usually made of metal with a small slider. This is great to use when marking a hem or trimming fabric from the bottom of a jacket, skirt or sleeve.

- - - - - - MARKING TOOLS - - - - - -

Marking Pencils: There are a variety of tools out there, from chalk pencils to air-soluble markers. I've recently discovered Sewline marking pencils. What can I say about these pencils? They're the best! They work like a mechanical pencil with a retractable lead and even come with a handy eraser that really does remove the marks from the fabric. They come in a variety of colors. I have tried many marking pencils over the years, and these are, hands-down, the best. These can be purchased at your local quilt shop or online.

- - - IRONS & IRONING BOARDS - - -

Irons: I have a Rowenta Steam Generator. If you do a lot of ironing, you need this tool. It has fantastic steam power which makes ironing so easy! It holds four cups of water in the tank, which is about 1½ solid hours of steam. This means you can pretty much sew all day and not run out of steam. How is that for awesome?

Ironing Board: I have a Rowenta Professional Ironing Board—I love this little beauty! It features an extra-wide board, making it a great location to lay out pieces to get them ready for ironing. It also has a shelf to the side for holding the iron and a lower shelf for holding other items. It's heavy duty and well balanced so that it does not tip easily.

CUTTING TOOLS

Scissors: I have three pairs of 6" Gingher scissors. I keep them stashed at different locations in my studio so that a pair is always handy. These are tough scissors that retain their sharpness for a long time and can cut through many layers of fabric at once. They have great points which help to clip curves and snip into seam allowances where needed.

Thread Snips: I love having a pair of thread snips by the machine to clip threads. They fit easily into your hand and are ergonomically friendly.

Rotary Cutter and Mat: I use my rotary cutter and mat all the time. These tools, along with a quilting ruler, really are the best way to cut accurate squares, rectangles and strips.

Seam Ripper: It is inevitable that you will need a seam ripper from time to time to do some "un-sewing." Not fun, but sometimes necessary. I also like to use these for opening buttonholes; be careful if you do—these are very sharp and can cut beyond the end of the buttonhole!

OTHER TOOLS

Point Turner: I use a bamboo skewer or an acrylic point turner to fully turn out pieces. Because both of these have a duller point than scissors, you're less likely to punch through a corner. I keep two or three acrylic point turners on hand in the studio at all times.

Pins and Magnetic Pin Cushion: I use a variety of different-sized safety pins to turn tubes of fabric right side out. A lot of people like to use different turning tools, but I prefer the good old safety pin for this task. And I always have a supply of dressmaker's pins on hand. I like the ones with the pearlized heads—they are extra-long and very sharp.

I love magnetic pin cushions! Be sure to have at least one. It's so easy to keep track of your straight pins this way. If any are on the floor, just use the cushion to pick them up.

Pattern Tracing Cloth: This is a nylon product that is translucent with a grid of dots spaced 1" apart. It's virtually impossible to tear, making it superior to using tissue scraps for tracing newly altered pattern pieces. You can write on it with pencil or pen and it can be gently pressed with low heat. It comes pre-packaged in 5-yard lengths or can be purchased by the yard and it is 36" wide.

Quality Sewing Thread: In order to do quality work, you must have quality materials, and thread is a very important component. Be sure to purchase a reputable brand. The better brands are stronger and smoother with very little lint. This means that your machine will stay cleaner and your stitches will look better. What's not to like? I stick with polyester thread, but if you prefer a blend of cotton and poly, that works too.

My favorite brands are Gutermann and Mettler.

Quality Machine Needles: It pays to purchase good quality machine needles from a reputable company. I exclusively use Schmetz needles. Keep a nice variety of needles on hand, too. I use size 14 the most, but I also keep stretch and denim weight needles around for special applications.

Lighting: Invest in a good full spectrum lamp for your sewing space. It makes such a difference to your eyes. Colors will be truer in this type of light as well.

Managing Your Time

What about time management and those dreaded unfinished projects? Time seems to be the quintessential question, doesn't it? None of us ever seems to have enough of it. What I can tell you is that you make time for the things you want to do, plain and simple. I know that we whine about not getting this or that completed, but think about it. A lot of times we are coming up with excuses to make ourselves feel better about not getting something finished. That might sound harsh, but I know it is true for me.

The *best* policy for making the most of your time is to be focused on the task at hand, and to use your time as wisely as possible as often as you can. I find that it always helps to set goals for myself, both short-term and long-term. For example, what kind of task do you think could be accomplished in as little as 15 minutes? The result might just surprise you. Whatever you do, don't approach a task by piddling away a few minutes here or there—if that is all the time you can make for a task, you will never realize the goals you've set for yourself.

I think one of the things that we do too often is bite off more than we can chew. Plan one project at a time, then work on it. Be sure that you really care about seeing the project all the way through before starting. If you are only lukewarm about it to begin with, chances are it will become another one of those unfinished beasts sitting and staring at you from the corner!

I know what you are thinking: "But I can't get rid of it! I spent all this money on it and I hate it now, but it is so wasteful to let it go!" Quite frankly, letting go of something you never intend to finish isn't wasteful at all. I think we all have the best of intentions when we start a project. The excitement is high, the thrill of the beginning is great, but then the work settles in or we hit a snag and we get busy with other things. I think the lesson here is to choose projects that you can visualize yourself actually completing and enjoying. Use this as your motivation to finish it.

Don't feel bad if you have unfinished projects. *We all do!* Just focus on how to end up with *fewer* incomplete projects. By looking at the real reasons we abandon projects to start with, we can eliminate wasted time, energy and supplies. To evaluate, ask yourself the following questions:

Could I change something about this project so I can get something from it?

Do I know someone who would love to have it under the condition that they finish and enjoy it?

Can I salvage the materials in this project and use them for something else?

It is best to unburden yourself and free up your space for more creative thoughts. As they say, "Out with the old, in with the new!" If you find yourself getting rid of a lot of old stuff, then think about how you can have a different outcome next time. I always try to make a change when I think something needs improving. I have a bad habit of holding on to fabric scraps after a project, so I have taken to donating them to folks who use them in quilts and other projects. It makes me feel good to know that those pieces will have life somewhere else, and it leaves me with room for more stuff, so it's all good!

Finally, always take some time to reflect. What kind of sewing goal would you like to set for yourself? Remember to start small with something that you know you can accomplish. How will you feel when you have realized this goal? Remember that reflection is important to growing and learning more about yourself, so don't skip it!

Sewing Patterns

SEWING WITH SERENDIPITY
Spring Fling Apron Pocket Template
Trace one onto freezer paper
Cut two from fabric
Cut one from interfacing
3/8" seam allowance included

ACTUAL SIZE

SEWING WITH SERENDIPITY
Spring Fling Apron Scallop Template
Trace one onto freezer paper
Cut 5 or 6 from fabric
1/2" seam allowance included

ACTUAL SIZE

For correctly sized
PDF templates
(and bonus photos!), visit
SewSerendipity.com/books

Place on Fold of Freezer Paper

Pocket Zipper Opening

SEWING WITH SERENDIPITY
Birdie Wristlet Pattern Template
Trace one on the fold to freezer paper
Transfer pocket zipper marking to ONE SIDE ONLY
1/2" seam allowance included

ENLARGE TEMPLATE BY 200%

Place on Fold

ENLARGE
TEMPLATE
BY 200%

SEWING WITH SERENDIPITY
Earwarmer Pattern Template
Trace one onto freezer paper
Cut one each from wool and fleece

ACTUAL SIZE

SEWING WITH SERENDIPITY
Earwarmer Pattern Template
Trace one onto freezer paper
Cut 6 from wool

Chapter One

SPRING

Ah, spring. What a lovely season! With trees budding, flowers blooming and birds bustling about, springtime always ushers in the promise of new beginnings. Surrounded by luscious new growth and vibrant pops of color, one can't help but feel excited about things to come!

Using the techniques discussed in this chapter—adding inset zippers, applying machine appliqué, choosing fabrics and using bias strips—you'll create two darling accessories that will help you carry around a bit of spring all year long! The Birdie Wristlet design is small and sweet, featuring fresh spring colors. This little bag is a cinch to stitch up and gives you an opportunity to show off a bit of appliqué with touches of beadwork here and there. The Spring Fling Apron has a retro appeal with its scalloped edges and rickrack, yet still looks fresh and modern with the choice of fabrics. This design is the ideal accessory to perk up a day spent in the kitchen cooking heavenly delights! And really, what could be better than that?

Spring Sewing Goals

This spring, I will:

_____
_____
_____
_____
_____

Classes I want to take:

_____
_____
_____
_____
_____

Techniques I want to master:

_____
_____
_____
_____
_____

Projects I intend to sew:

_____
_____
_____
_____

SPRING CHECKLIST

Items I need to purchase for my projects:

_____
_____
_____
_____

Gifts to Sew This Season

Item:

For: on the occasion of

Started:

Notions needed:

Materials needed:

Notes:

Item:

For: on the occasion of

Started:

Notions needed:

Materials needed:

Notes:

Item:

For: on the occasion of

Started:

Notions needed:

Materials needed:

Notes:

Item:

For: on the occasion of

Started:

Notions needed:

Materials needed:

Notes:

Sewing Advice
Zip It Up! Adding an Inset Zipper

I can't tell you how often people get freaked out when I mention sewing in a zipper! Zippers make wonderful closures, and once you know how simple it is to install an inset zipper, you will feel silly that you were ever intimidated by one.

Inset zippers can be added to all sorts of projects such as bag exteriors or interiors, jackets, skirt fronts or even notebook covers. What's more, you can install them vertically, horizontally or even on an angle, allowing for great versatility in your sewing projects. The following tutorial will take you through the process step by step to show you just how simple inset zippers really are!

1   The first thing to do when installing an inset zipper is to take a look at where you want the zipper to go. For a bag, it is best to center it along one side of an exterior or interior with some space to either side of it. Decide on an approximate length for the zipper you will need.

Next, purchase the zipper you want to use. You can buy one that is exactly the length you need with a closed bottom (meaning it will not separate, like one for a jacket) or it can be a little longer than what you need in the event that the exact length you need is not available. Once the zipper has been sewn in place, the extra length can be cut away.

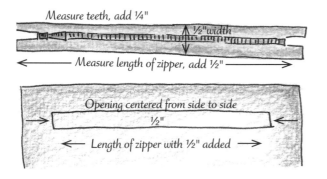

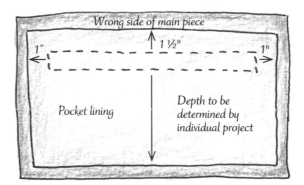

2   Measure across the width of the zipper teeth and add about ¼". Add ½" to the desired length for the zipper. On the wrong side of the piece that you want to add the zipper to, mark the zipper length with the extra ½" added, centered from side to side, then mark the width with the ¼" added. You will be creating a long, skinny rectangle, which will become the opening for the zipper to fit into. For most sport type zippers, the width of the opening will need to be ½".

3   The inset zipper will be an opening to a concealed pocket, so the next thing you will need to do is create a pocket lining. Measure 1" to either side of the rectangle and 1½" above. The depth of the pocket will depend on the size of the piece you are adding it to, as well as your personal preference for the pocket. Cut two rectangles this size.

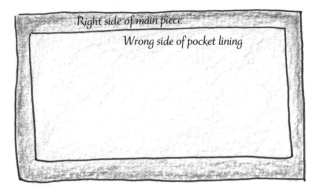

Right side of main piece

Wrong side of pocket lining

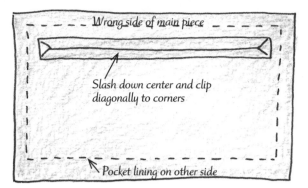

Wrong side of main piece

Slash down center and clip diagonally to corners

Pocket lining on other side

4 Place one of the rectangles against the right side of the piece where the zipper will be installed, centered, and with the top edge 1½" above the center of the marked rectangle. Pin in place.

5 Stitch the two pieces together with the wrong side facing up where you have marked the rectangle. Stitch directly on top of the marking that has been made. Once the rectangle has been stitched, slash through all layers of fabric through the center and snip diagonally to all corners.

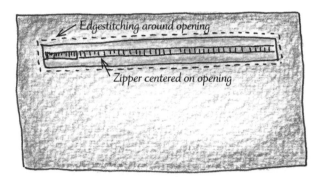

Edgestitching around opening

Zipper centered on opening

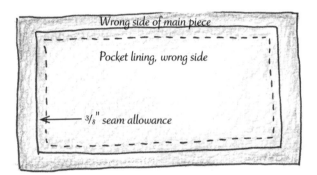

Wrong side of main piece

Pocket lining, wrong side

3/8" seam allowance

6 Turn the lining through the rectangle to the other side and press the stitched edges along the seam, making sure that the lining is completely concealed at the opening. The opening for the zipper is now complete.

Add the zipper from the back so that it shows through the opening and is centered. Use temporary spray adhesive or pins to secure it in place, and use a zipper foot to attach the zipper, edgestitching along the finished edge all the way around. Use caution when stitching over the zipper teeth so as not to break the needle if your zipper is longer than needed. Once the stitching is complete, trim down the zipper if it was longer than what was needed for the opening.

7 Add the remaining pocket lining to the piece already attached, right sides together. Using a ⅜" seam allowance, stitch the two lining pieces together, holding it away from the main piece. You should now have an inset zipper installed with a concealed pocket behind it. See? It was super simple!

Sewing Advice
Working With Machine Appliqué

Adding appliqué detail is a great way to punch up the interest of a project. It is also a wonderful way to personalize a gift by adding a monogram or something that is special to the recipient. I personally love to work with machine appliqué. It is so easy to do, especially when working with non-fraying fabrics such as felt. There are so many lovely colors of felt that you can find one to work with any fabric.

Appliqué also lends itself very well to embellishment. Once it is added, you can finish with your own personal accents, such as beads and trims or hand embroidery. Buttons sewn to the centers of flowers are a pretty and easy accent as well. Just remember: Adding appliqué needs to happen early in a project, before too much construction has occurred. This way, you have easy access to where you want the design to be. Also be sure to keep seam allowances in mind when adding appliqué to an unfinished project to guarantee proper placement.

- - - · FUSIBLE MACHINE APPLIQUÉ · - - -

When working with machine appliqué where you want to secure all of the edges, it is much easier when a fusible product such as HeatnBond is used. This keeps the pieces of your appliqué in place until they are stitched. Be sure to purchase the "lite" version since the no-sew version can do seriously scary things to your sewing machine. The adhesive can carry through the machine's inner parts and gum it up, so avoid that no-sew stuff!

There are a few things to keep in mind when adding a fusible product to fabric. Since felt has no right or wrong side, you will not need to be mindful of which side is used, but if you use a fabric that has an obvious right or wrong side, be sure to add the fusible product to the wrong side.

1 Trace the design onto the paper portion of the fusible product. Keep in mind that any design you choose will be the *reverse image* since you are adding it to the wrong side of fabric. This means that initials will need to be backwards and any other images such as a bird will be facing the opposite direction once added to the project.

2 After the design is traced, cut around the design and leave a margin that will be cut away later. Add the fusible piece to the wrong side of the fabric with the paper side facing upward. Press to fuse the fusible to the fabric, then cut along the drawn edges to cut out the appliqué.

3 Carefully peel away the paper backing and add the fusible side of the appliqué to the right side of fabric on your project. Once you are pleased with the placement, press the appliqué to fuse it in place.

4 Now you can stitch around the edges of the appliqué. You have several choices for how to stitch around the design: Use a small straight stitch just inside the cut edge all the way around; use a small blanket stitch; or use a narrow satin stitch (a tight zigzag stitch).

A Note About Thread

I love to use rayon machine embroidery thread (such as Sulky) for machine appliqué. It adds a subtle sheen to the stitches and gives an overall lovely result. If appliqué is new to you, you might want to practice a bit on scraps before doing the actual stitching on your project to get comfortable with the process, to get to know your machine and to discover the look you like best with different stitches.

- DIMENSIONAL MACHINE APPLIQUÉ -

What if you do not want to secure the edges of the appliqué and want a more open textural feel? I only recommend this method with fabrics that will not fray, such as felted wool or felt. To make the process easier, I recommend purchasing some freezer paper which can be found in the grocery store alongside foil and other food storage items. It comes on a roll and is paper with a plastic coating on one side. This plastic coating is perfect because it will temporarily stick to fabric when pressed, then peel away once you have cut out your pieces. The best part is that the paper can be used over and over as the plastic side will continue to adhere to fabric many times.

To use freezer paper, trace the design onto the paper on the dull side. Cut out the design on the drawn lines. Press the shiny side down onto the right side of the fabric, then cut out the shape. Peel away the paper, and the appliqué is ready to be added to the project.

I recommend this method for shapes like leaves and flowers where you want the edges to be free. For leaves, just stitch down the center and add a few veins if you like. For flowers, stitch the center in place. You can even layer several flower shapes together for a "fluffier" flower result. This is also a lovely technique for adding wings to a bird appliqué. You could stitch part of the wing and leave the rest open.

A Note About Machine Feet

I highly recommend the use of an open-toe embroidery foot for appliqué. This allows you to see where the needle is at all times. This is paramount when you are pivoting around the edges of small pieces.

Spring Sewing Project
Birdie Wristlet

FABRICS

⅓ yd. Fabric A for bag exterior

⅓ yd. Fabric B for bag interior, ring tabs and handle

⅙ yd. Fabric C for pocket lining

WoolFelt in assorted colors:

> 4" square Color A for birds
>
> 6" × 3" piece Color B for branch
>
> 3" square Color C for flowers
>
> 3" square Color D for leaves

STABILIZERS

13" × 15" piece Roc-Lon Multi-Purpose Cloth for bag exterior

4" × 8" piece HeatnBond Lite for appliqué pieces

½ yd. Pellon 911FF lightweight fusible interfacing for bag interior

Temporary adhesive spray such as Sulky KK #2000 or 505

NOTIONS

¾" metal O-rings × 2

¾" swivel clasp

9" vinyl sport zippers × 2

Beading needle (as needed)

Beads of various sizes and colors for appliqué embellishment

Fabric marking pencil such as Sewline

Freezer paper to make bag template

Polyester thread to match fabrics

Rotary cutter, ruler and mat

Sulky rayon machine embroidery thread for appliqué pieces

Zipper foot

Zipper pull (optional)

What better way to welcome the arrival of spring than with an adorable wristlet bag? This one is perfect when you need to carry just the essentials with you. It is created from one pattern piece with the ingenious addition of two inset zippers. This enables you to have a few things nicely organized within a fingertip's reach, yet completely enclosed with the security of the zippers. This little bag would be fabulous to carry to a spring wedding or other special occasion. What a great gift it would make for one lucky gal!

A Note About Multi-Purpose Cloth

Multi-Purpose cloth is *not* a fusible stabilizer. It looks like an artist's canvas and is used often to make area rugs and other items. It is also known as *blackout*, as it can be used to block light on windows. I highly recommend this product, as it has nice body and is super easy to work with. It can be purchased by the yard online or in local fabric stores. Some outlets have it precut in one yard pieces as well.

The finished bag is 7" wide x 5" tall, and is 2" deep at the base and 1" deep at the top edge. The handle can be used as a loop or small handle, depending on how the swivel clasp is attached. The handle is roughly 15" long, including the hardware.

- - - - PREPARING THE TEMPLATE - - - -

1 Trace the pattern on page 11 onto freezer paper, transferring the placement for zippers, then cut out. Also cut out the small rectangles for the zipper placement. Note: The pattern piece included is ON THE FOLD. When making the template, be sure to place the fold of the pattern piece onto a folded piece of freezer paper so that the piece can be opened out after cutting.

Fold of freezer paper

Pattern template

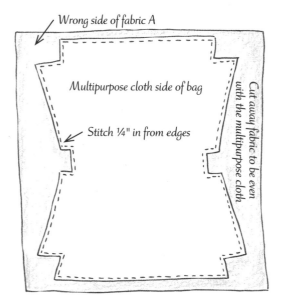

Wrong side of fabric A

Multipurpose cloth side of bag

Stitch ¼" in from edges

Cut away fabric to be even with the multipurpose cloth

Pattern template pressed to multipurpose cloth side

Trace zipper opening for pocket ONLY

- - - - - MAKING THE BAG EXTERIOR - - - - -

1 Place the template paper right side up onto the Multi-Purpose Cloth and stick the two together temporarily by lightly pressing. Cut around the outside edges, then peel away the template.

2 Lightly spray one side of the Multi-Purpose Cloth, then add Fabric A right side facing up on top and smooth out the fabric. Pin together, then flip over and stitch ¼" in from all the edges, following the Multi-Purpose Cloth. Trim the fabric to be even with the edge of the cloth once stitching is complete.

3 On the Multi-Purpose Cloth side, reattach the freezer paper template by lightly pressing in place. Trace the zipper opening for the pocket, then peel away the template.

4 Cut two 5" × 8" rectangles from Fabric C for the pocket lining. On the fabric side of the bag exterior (the same side that the zipper opening is marked on the stabilizer), center the fabric, right sides together, and pin in place.

5 Flip the piece over so that the zipper opening is visible. Follow steps in the Inset Zipper article on pages 16–17 to install the zipper.

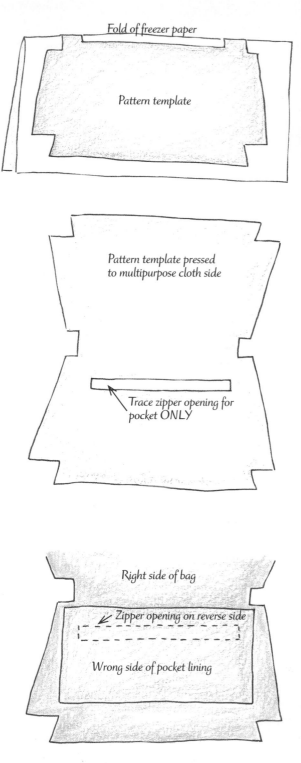

Right side of bag

Zipper opening on reverse side

Wrong side of pocket lining

Adding Visual Interest

To add a bit of extra interest, I hand stitched some decorative beads
to the birds, flower centers and branch.

--- --- ADDING THE APPLIQUÉ - --- -

1 Add the appliqué pieces to the other side of the bag exterior following the instructions on page 18. Beginning with the branch, place the appliqué pieces on one at a time and stitch them down as you go (the branch placement should be about 2½" down from the finished zipper). Next, add the birds, flowers and leaves. Use a small machine blanket stitch for the branch and birds; stitch down the centers of the leaves using a straight machine stitch; and stitch outward from the centers with a straight stitch in a contrasting thread color for the flowers.

BAG INTERIOR AND TOP ZIPPER INSTALLATION

1 Adhere the freezer paper template to Fabric B and cut out around the outside edges. Peel away the template. Place the fabric onto the fusible interfacing with the wrong side of the fabric against the fusible side of the interfacing and cut out. Fuse together following the manufacturer's instructions.

2 Place the template on top of the interfacing side of the piece and press to stick together. Trace the rectangle for the top zipper, then peel away the template.

3 Place the bag interior on top of the bag exterior, right sides together with edges even. Follow the steps on pages 16–17 to stitch the opening. Once the opening is complete, pin the outer edges together before adding the zipper to keep the fabric in place.

Add the zipper following steps on page 17, making sure that both zippers zip in the same direction. Unpin the outer edges of the exterior and interior and set bag aside.

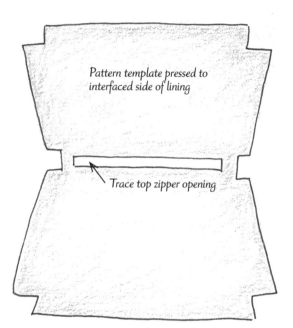

Pattern template pressed to interfaced side of lining

Trace top zipper opening

--- --- PREPARING THE HANDLE AND RING TABS - --- -

1 Cut a 2" × 20" strip from Fabric B and fusible interfacing. Fuse the interfacing to the wrong side of the strip. Then, fold the fabric in half, wrong sides together, so that it is 1" wide and press. Open out the strip and fold the outer edges toward the fold and press, then fold in half along the center once more and press. Edgestitch both long edges.

1"

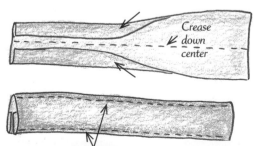

Crease down center

Edgestitching

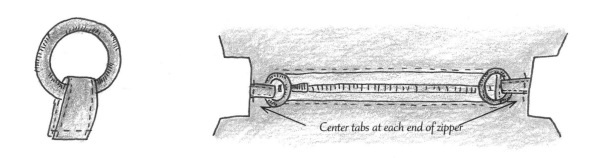

Center tabs at each end of zipper

2 From this piece, cut two 2" pieces for the ring tabs, reserving the remainder for the handle.

Place each 2" piece through an O-ring and fold in half. Stitch across the ends, ¼" from the edge.

3 Center the tabs at each end of the top zipper on the bag exterior. The bag interior should be pinned out of the way before stitching the tabs in place. Stitch across the end of each tab to attach.

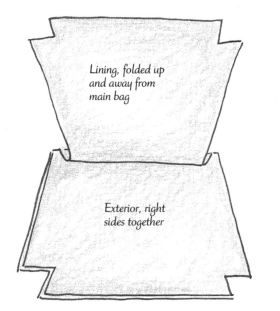

Lining, folded up and away from main bag

Exterior, right sides together

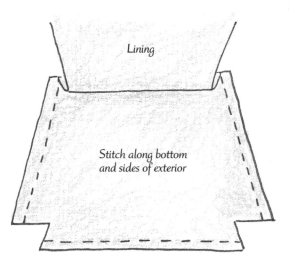

Lining

Stitch along bottom and sides of exterior

- - - SEWING THE BAG TOGETHER - - -

1 Unzip the top zipper at this time. It is not necessary to completely unzip it, but open it enough that you can pull the lining through in a later step. Then, fold the bag in half so that the exterior portions are right sides together. The bag interior should be free of these pieces at this time.

2 Pin the edges together and stitch along the bottom edge with a ½" seam allowance. Also, sew the side seams. I find it helpful to use a zipper foot to sew the side seams, since you will be stitching close to the ends of the zipper at the top of the bag.

3 Trim down the seams to ¼", then open out the bottom corners to align the side and lower seams to form the corners of the bag. Bring these together and stitch with a ½" seam, then trim down to ¼".

4 Open out the same way at the top corners, ensuring that the ring tab is lying flat, and stitch across. Trim down the seam.

5 Repeat this process for the bag interior, but leave an opening along the bottom edge for turning right side out. DO NOT stitch the top corners. It is too difficult to get to them. They will be hand-stitched closed in a later step.

6 Turn the interior right side out through the bottom opening. This will cause the interior to enclose the bag exterior. Stitch the bottom opening closed as well as the top corners, then turn the entire bag right side out through the top zipper opening.

Fully open out the corners and press as necessary to get the layers to fit to one another. See the article on page 48 for more details.

Using the remaining handle piece, place one end through the swivel clasp. Turn under the raw edge by ¼" or so to conceal and stitch in place as illustrated.

7 Place the other end of the handle through the O-ring on the bag that is nearest the zipper pulls, and finish off the end as in step 6. Then add the zipper pull to the pocket zipper.

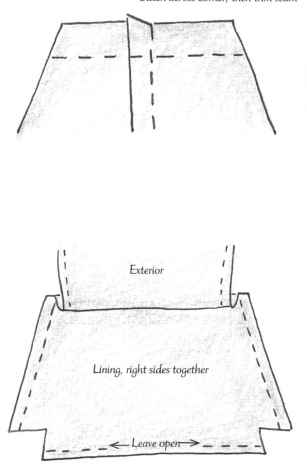

Stitch across corner, then trim seam

Exterior

Lining, right sides together

← Leave open →

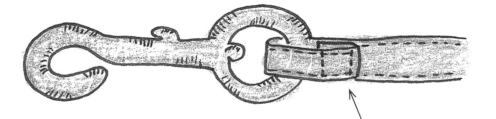

Fold in end, then stitch in place

Time for Reflection

What did you like best about this project?

_____

_____

_____

_____

_____

_____

_____

What would you do differently next time?

_____

_____

_____

_____

_____

_____

_____

_____

What new skill did you learn and how do you plan on using
these on other projects?

_____

_____

_____

_____

_____

_____

_____

Decisions, Decisions! Choosing Fabrics

Selecting the right fabrics can seem daunting. How do you know what goes together or what to put where on a project? Of course, a lot depends on personal taste, but what if you still find yourself struggling with choosing fabrics? Below are several factors I consider when selecting my own fabrics. You can use these pointers as a guide to help you get started!

First, pay attention to which fabrics catch your eye. Why do you like the fabric? Is it color, pattern, texture or theme that interests you most? In analyzing what you like about different fabrics, you can begin to see what in particular drives your interest. Color often moves me the most. I love vibrant color and find it particularly eye-catching when combined with a large-scale design. I think fabric should always make a bold statement.

Next, try to visualize the project made in the fabric you like. If it is an article of clothing, drape the fabric across your body and look in the mirror. This can help you see if it will look the way you've pictured in your mind. If the fabric is for a bag or another accessory, try standing away from the fabric to see what kind of impact it has. If the print has a small motif, you may realize the pattern you liked up close disappears and reads as a solid from a distance. If you want a print that makes impact, you may have to adjust your choice to a fabric with a larger motif or greater contrast.

Once you know what you like about a particular fabric, begin looking for other fabrics that enhance its unique qualities. See what a smaller, more graphic print would do when added with a larger scale fabric in a contrasting color. It is helpful to lay the fabrics together with the dominant fabric on top and tuck the other fabrics in around the edge to see how they interact with the main fabric. It is good for each fabric to have an opportunity to make a contribution to the project. If any two fabrics blend into one another too much, you lose the effect of using more than one.

In general, I use large-scale fabrics on the largest pieces of a project to allow it to dominate. These types of fabrics work best in this role because the less they are cut into smaller pieces, the more the motif stays intact and maintains impact. Think of the other fabrics as having a supporting role in the process. Prints with stripes or dots, or even a smaller scale of the dominant print, bring interest without competing.

You will notice I chose to work within one fabric collection for several of the projects in this book. When starting out, this is a great way to build your confidence in putting fabrics together. I often work within one collection because I can find all of the prints I need without having to mix and match between collections. This is especially helpful if you are purchasing fabric online. Computer monitors often distort the value of a color, and you may be disappointed when you see the fabric in person. If you live near a local shop, visit in person to mix and match between different manufacturers. This also eliminates the risks associated with online shopping. You never know what may strike you until the fabric is right before your eyes!

To get comfortable with choosing fabrics, keep it simple. Choose only two or three fabrics and plan for a simple project that is not a huge investment of time. This way, you get quick results and see how you did with your choices.

Finally, remember to reflect upon your experience once the project is complete. Are you happy with your choices? If so, why do you think it worked as well as it did? If not, what could you have done differently? This is something that I have mentally done many times over the years. The more you practice this skill and evaluate your results, the easier it will get.

Sewing Advice
Cutting and Using Bias Strips

Quite often in sewing, fabric is cut on the bias, but why? Won't a regular strip work just the same? In a word, no! Cutting diagonally across the grain increases the stretch of the fabric. This is especially helpful when working with wovens such as cotton, silk or wool, where the fabric needs to accommodate a curved edge.

Keep in mind that not all curved edges are going to be along the edge of a bag flap, pillow, quilt or edge of clothing. Sometimes cutting fabric on the bias makes it fit better against the body, such as for a waistband. This extra stretch allows the fabric to conform and fit snugly, as is the case with the *Spring Fling Apron* project.

When working with fabric that has been cut on the bias, it is important to handle the fabric carefully. Because there is the added element of stretch, you can experience some edge distortion if the fabric is pulled too tightly. It is always best to pin the edges to be sewn together to eliminate the possibility of distorting the fabric.

Cutting fabric on the bias is very simple to do and only requires a few tools. I like to use scissors to get the first cut and then continue with my rotary cutter and mat. The ends are then sewn together and pressed to create a long strip that can then be used as a binding or other flexible piece in a project.

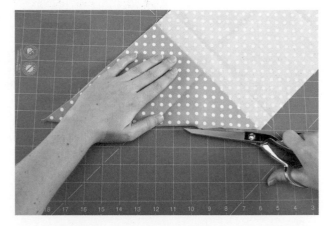

1 To cut on the bias, begin by folding up a corner on the diagonal and trimming it off.

2 Fold the fabric along this newly cut edge.

3 Using a rotary cutter, cut the strips to a specified width according to your project instructions. Cut however many strips it will take to go around the piece you are binding.

4 Place the ends of the strips together at a 90-degree angle. Piece the strips right sides together along the angled edges with a ¼" seam allowance.

5 Trim off the points.

6 Press the seams open.

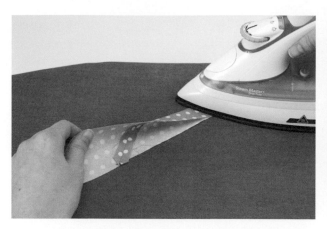

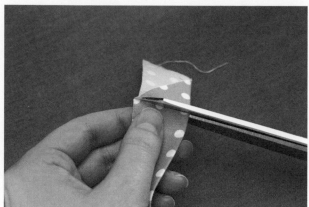

7 Fold the strip in half lengthwise with wrong sides together and press.

8 Trim the angled seam edges to straighten.

9 Open out the strip once more. Fold the narrow edge back ½" to the wrong side and press.

10 Fold the strip in half lengthwise with wrong sides together once more and press briefly. Add the bias strip as directed in the project instructions.

Be a domestic diva with this sweet little apron that is a snap to sew together! Pick six coordinating fabrics and you are ready to sew. Because it is composed of tapered panels, it has a gentle A-line shape that is complimentary to everyone. There is even an option to add an extra panel to make the apron wider if you like. The addition of a bias tie makes for a nice close fit to the body, and the addition of some wide rickrack lends a nice retro vibe to this project.

Spring Sewing Project

Spring Fling Apron

FABRICS

½ yd. Fabric A for main apron panels

⅛ yd. Fabric B for scallops

¼ yd. Fabric C for pocket

2" strip Fabric D for pocket ruffle

⅝ yd. Fabric E for apron back

½ yd. Fabric F for apron tie

1½ yd. ¾" wide rickrack or other flexible trim

STABILIZERS

⅛ yd. Pellon 911FF lightweight fusible interfacing

NOTIONS

Freezer or plain paper to make pattern templates

Marking pencil such as Sewline

Polyester thread to match fabrics

Rotary cutter, ruler and mat

Ruffler foot (optional)

Adjusting the Length of Your Apron

What if you want to make a longer apron? Since the requirement is ½ yard, you have the option to cut the panels up to 3" longer, which would result in an apron measuring about 21" long. If you want one longer than that, increase the fabric requirement to more than ½ yard.

The finished five-panel apron measures 20" wide at the top, 24" wide at the bottom edge and is 18" long (including width of tie). The six-panel version measures 24" wide at the top, 28" wide at the bottom edge and is 18" long.

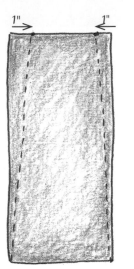

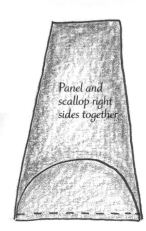

Panel and scallop right sides together

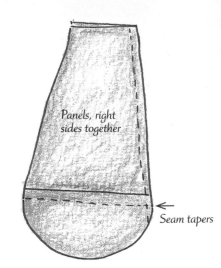

Panels, right sides together

← *Seam tapers*

CUTTING AND SEWING THE MAIN APRON PANELS

1 Cut 5 or 6 panels from Fabric A measuring 6" × 15". Taper the top edge of each panel by 1" using a rotary cutter, ruler and mat.

2 Decide on the order of the panels, then number them on the wrong side of the fabric in the order you would like to stitch them.

3 Trace the scallop pattern on page 11 to freezer paper and cut out. Cut 5 or 6 scallops from Fabric B.

4 Add a scallop to the bottom edge of each apron panel, right sides together. Pin, then stitch together with a ½" seam allowance. Press each seam toward the apron panel.

5 Stitch the panels together in numerical order, right sides together, with a ½" seam allowance. Note that the seam allowance will taper off as the scallop is stitched. Press the seams open.

ADDING THE POCKET

1 Trace the pocket pattern on page 11 to freezer or plain paper and cut out. Cut two pockets from Fabric C and one from interfacing. Fuse the interfacing to the wrong side of one of the pocket pieces.

2 Fold the 2" strip of Fabric D in half, wrong sides together, so that it measures 1" in width. Press. Ruffle the strip by using a ruffler foot attachment set at every stitch, ¼" from the raw edges, or using a long straight machine stitch, complete two rows of gathering stitches ¼" and ⅜" away from the raw edges and pull up bobbin threads to gather. Press the ruffle flat.

3 To add the ruffle to the top of the pocket, turn back one end of the ruffle by ¼" twice to conceal the raw edge. Add it to the top of the interfaced pocket piece along the right side of fabric starting ⅜" in from the side edge. Pin across the top edge of the pocket, then trim down the length so that enough remains to turn back the edge inside the seam allowance. Stitch in place ⅜" from the edge.

4 Add the remaining pocket piece right sides together and pin the edges together. Leave an opening along the top edge for turning. Stitch together with a ⅜" seam allowance. The ruffle should remain free from the side seams. Clip the corners diagonally and wedge clip the curves.

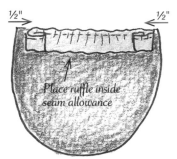

½"   ½"

Place ruffle inside seam allowance

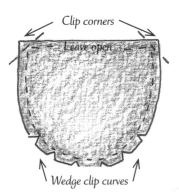

Clip corners

Leave open

Wedge clip curves

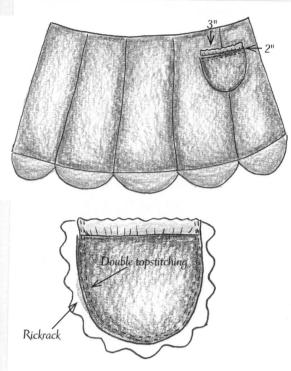

3"

2"

5 Turn the pocket right side out, fully turning out the curve and top corners. Turn the ruffle out so that it stands above the pocket and press. Turn under the opening edge and press, then double topstitch the top edge of the pocket.

6 Place the pocket onto the apron panels along the left side (during wear), 2" in from the side edge and 3" down from the top edge to the top of the ruffle. Pin in place.

Double topstitching

Rickrack

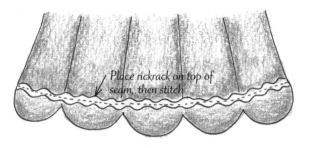

Place rickrack on top of seam, then stitch

7 Slip the rickrack underneath the pocket's finished edge so that one half of it is showing, starting at one of the top edges at the ruffle. Turn under the edge of the rickrack, then pin in place all the way around until the other top edge is reached. Turn under the edge of the rickrack once more.

8 Stitch the edge of the pocket in place starting at the top of the ruffle and edgestitching first, then topstitching ¼" from the edge.

9 Add rickrack on top of the seam where the scallops join the main panels. Stitch down the center of the trim.

Leave top open

Wedge clip curves before turning

Pivot at each scallop

Edgestitching

Stitch top edge closed

Double topstitch edges

- - - - ADDING THE APRON BACK - - - -

1 Lay the main apron piece right sides together on top of Fabric D. Pin together, then trim the backing fabric even with the edges of the main apron piece.

2 Stitch the front and back together with a ½" seam along the sides and scalloped edge. The front should be facing upward so that the scallop seams can be followed for accurate pivoting of the seam.

3 Wedge clip the scallops and clip to each pivot between the scallops. Turn right side out, fully turning out the scallops and press. Stitch the top edge together ¼" from the raw edges.

4 Edgestitch down each seam on both sides, skipping around the pocket. Double topstitch the finished edges of the apron.

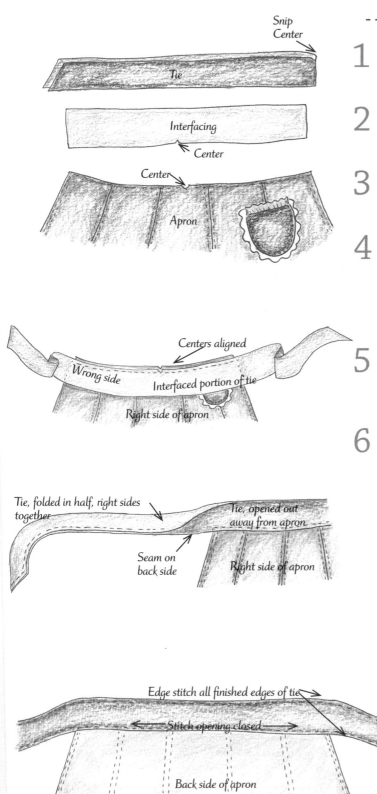

Snip Center

Tie

Interfacing

Center

Center

Apron

Centers aligned

Wrong side

Interfaced portion of tie

Right side of apron

Tie, folded in half, right sides together

Tie, opened out away from apron

Seam on back side

Right side of apron

Edge stitch all finished edges of tie

Stitch opening closed

Back side of apron

1 Cut a series of 6" wide strips from Fabric E following the bias cutting technique on page 29. You will need about 100" in length.

2 Once the strips have been sewn together and pressed, cut a piece of interfacing measuring 6" × 20" or 24", depending on the version of apron being made.

3 Mark the center of the tie by folding it in half and snipping the fold. Do the same for the interfacing as well as the top of the apron.

4 Fuse the interfacing to the wrong side of the tie, matching centers. Add the tie to the apron, right sides together matching centers. Stitch together with a ½" seam allowance across the top of the apron. Open out the tie away from the main apron piece and press the seam toward the tie.

5 Fold the tie right sides together to either side of the apron and stitch together with a ½" seam allowance. Trim the angle of the ends so that they match before stitching.

6 Clip the points of the seam allowance at the ends of the tie, then turn each one right side out. Fully turn out the points, then press. Press under the seam allowance along the tie where it lies on top of the apron. Pin in place, then double topstitch the edges of the tie.

To wear the apron, cross the ties in back and bring them around to the front and tie in a bow or knot.

" Time for Reflection

What did you learn about fabric placement in this project?

_____

_____

_____

_____

_____

Is there a fabric that you would have put in a different place? If so, why?

_____

_____

_____

_____

_____

What other ideas would you add for embellishing this apron if you were to make another one?

_____

_____

_____

_____

_____

Is there a different trim or perhaps decorative ribbon you could add?

_____

_____

_____

_____

_____

"

NOTES

Chapter Two
SUMMER

Summertime, and the livin' is easy. There is just something about the laid-back feel of a lazy summer day. The projects featured in this chapter perfectly capture that relaxed summer attitude, getting you in the mood for leisurely strolls and Sunday afternoon picnics.

The articles in this chapter cover hand embroidery, sewing and pressing, working with color, and adding binding. Having a handle on these skills will help you create the whimsical summer skirt and picnic quilt showcased in this chapter, no doubt yielding fabulous results! What's more, the use of precut fabrics makes the projects even easier. Not only will you save time picking out fabric, but you won't have to cut as much either, which means you can spend more time on planning fabric placement and sewing … and enjoying the beautiful summer weather, of course!

Summer Sewing Goals

This summer, I will: _____
_____
_____
_____
_____
_____

Classes I want to take: _____
_____
_____
_____
_____

Techniques I want to master: _____
_____
_____
_____
_____
_____

Projects I intend to sew: _____
_____
_____
_____
_____
_____

SUMMER CHECKLIST

Items I need to purchase for my projects:
_____
_____
_____
_____

Gifts to Sew This Season

Item:

For: on the occasion of

Started:

Notions needed:

Materials needed:

Notes:

Item:

For: on the occasion of

Started:

Notions needed:

Materials needed:

Notes:

Item:

For: on the occasion of

Started:

Notions needed:

Materials needed:

Notes:

Item:

For: on the occasion of

Started:

Notions needed:

Materials needed:

Notes:

Sewing Advice
The Charm of Hand Embroidery

I love the little extra something that hand embroidery brings to a project, not to mention it is amazingly easy to learn. When I was a girl, hand embroidery was the first sewing skill my mother taught me. I think it is a great way to get young stitchers excited because there are so many colors of floss to use, yet the supplies and instructions stay simple. Perhaps this is why there's been such a resurgence of embroidery among designers today. It seems like everywhere you look, there are little hand-stitched accents on everything!

Another bonus to this technique is that embroidery supplies are easily accessible and mostly affordable, too. All you need is a hand needle and embroidery floss or thread to get started. You can get fancy with all sorts of silk and hand-dyed threads, but you're under no obligation to do so. Simple embroidery floss works just fine. You can also use Pearl cotton if you prefer. It comes in a variety of weights and is only one strand, so there is no need to separate it into individual strands.

There are several things to keep in mind when working with embroidery floss:

✧ Most floss is 6-stranded. For most applications, I use 2–3 threads of floss at one time, so you will need to separate the individual strands and use however many you desire at one time. For the projects in this book, I state how many strands have been used as a guideline.

✧ Keep the length of the floss 24" or shorter. Anything longer than that tends to twist and tangle, and then you spend most of your time fighting with the floss ... not fun!

✧ If you like, you can use an embroidery hoop to keep the fabric stretched tight while stitching. This will help your stitches lie flat once the fabric has been released from the hoop. Personally, I use a hoop for cross stitching but not for embroidery. With a bit of practice on your stitching tension, you won't need to hoop your fabric either. However, in the end, it comes down to your preference.

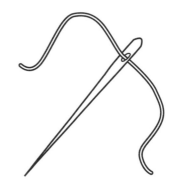

To get started, you will need the most basic of skills: Threading a hand needle. It is best to use needles that are specified for hand embroidery. These are usually short needles with a large eye so multiple strands are easily threaded and no stress is put on the thread itself.

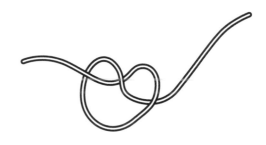

Next, you will need to know how to make a knot. For most applications, knotting your thread is perfectly acceptable. If you get into counted cross stitch, most stitchers skip the knotting in favor of leaving a longer tail on the backside of the work. This is usually because many cross stitch projects are framed and it is best to keep the work as flat as possible.

A Note About Stitches

Most stitches are easy to learn. The ones I like the best are backstitch, lazy daisy, chain, running stitch, satin stitch and French knots.

- ✧ When stitching a design, it is best not to carry your threads along the back of the work for very long stretches of space. It will be messy on the back and could show from the front.
- ✧ Remember that when you are ready to fasten off one color and move to another, take a few small stitches through the back of other stitches on the wrong side of the work to secure the end, then snip the remaining thread.
- ✧ If you are purchasing cotton floss that has a color number, I recommend purchasing the little flat spools to which you can transfer the floss along with the brand and the number. That way, if you run out, you know what it is and where to get more.
- ✧ As a general rule, if you are stitching on something that will likely be washed at any time, it is best to color treat the dark and bright colors to prevent bleeding. Soak the individual colors in very warm water with a bit of white vinegar. Once the dye stops bleeding, fully rinse it and allow it to air dry. Now it's ready for stitching.
- ✧ Once you have finished a piece of embroidery, lightly press it from the wrong side. This smooths out your stitches and lends a nice crisp appearance. If your piece contains a lot of French knots, it is best to place it face down on a towel before pressing so you don't flatten these areas.
- ✧ You can stitch on just about any type of fabric that you want. Traditionally, most work is completed on cotton or linen, but feel free to stitch on wool, denim, twill, velveteen—there really are no limits. If you can get a needle through it, stitch on it!
- ✧ When stitching on white cotton, I like to add a woven stabilizer to the back to make the fabric slightly thicker and less transparent. That way if you carry your thread to another stitch area, the carry will not show through to the right side.

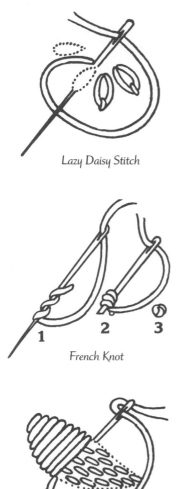

Lazy Daisy Stitch

French Knot

Satin Stitch

Different Types of Embroidery

Selecting a Design

There are so many ways to obtain the perfect design for your project. You can choose to draw your own designs, taking inspiration from a fabric that you are working with. If you're not comfortable drawing, you can purchase designs ready for stitching that can be traced or ironed onto fabrics. Or, if you are really feeling confident, you can freeform stitch and see where your creativity takes you!

A Place to Practice

If you're still feeling a little apprehensive about adding hand-drawn designs to your projects, there's no better way to remedy this than with practice! Below, I've chosen two of my favorite embellishments—birds and flowers—to illustrate just how easy adding hand-drawn designs can be. Use the blank page to the right to practice and perfect your own technique!

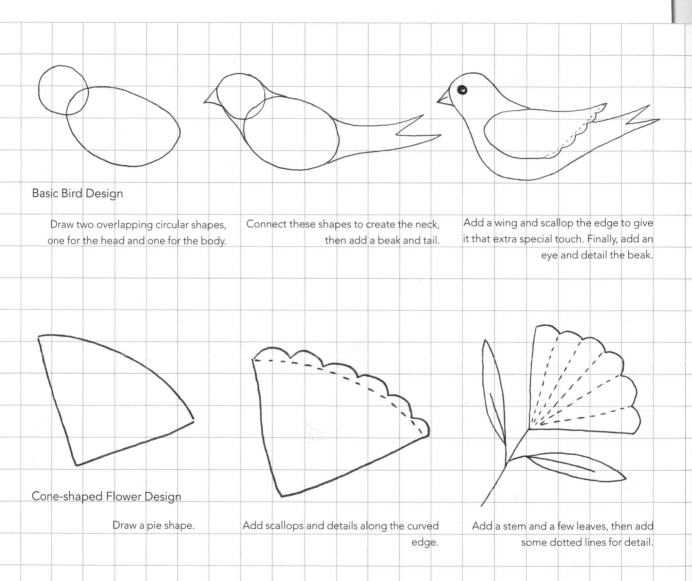

Basic Bird Design

Draw two overlapping circular shapes, one for the head and one for the body.

Connect these shapes to create the neck, then add a beak and tail.

Add a wing and scallop the edge to give it that extra special touch. Finally, add an eye and detail the beak.

Cone-shaped Flower Design

Draw a pie shape.

Add scallops and details along the curved edge.

Add a stem and a few leaves, then add some dotted lines for detail.

Sewing Advice
Pressing Matters

When sewing, it is always important to remember that the iron is one of your very best friends! It makes your stitching crisper and your finished project more professional. I like to use an iron with plenty of steam output. I have purchased a steam generator with an iron attached to the unit to get the highest possible output of steam with my sewing. This, of course, is my personal preference. Just be sure that when you purchase an iron, you get the best one you can afford and that it has adequate steam production. You will be much happier with the end result in the long run.

Whenever I press a seam, I will either press it open or to one side. By far, I press more seams to one side than I do open. Open seams are usually for fabrics that do not fray or if an item is going to be lined like a jacket. In this case, pressing the seam open will result in less bulk, and because they will be covered with a lining, it makes no difference to the appearance upon completion.

If the interior seams are to be exposed, I prefer to serge them so they don't fray during wear or wash. If you don't have a serger, use an overlock-type stitch on your conventional machine to secure the raw edges. Having said this, if you are piecing fabrics together for a quilt top, it is not necessary to finish the seam edges

since the quilt will have batting and a backing added, thus concealing those interior seams.

Once the stitching for a seam is complete, it is always best to press the seam. If you press as you go, your finished project will be far better than if you wait until the end to press. In a lot of instances, you will never be able to attain the finished result you want if you do not press enough during the sewing process.

If you do any degree of garment or bag sewing, it is helpful to purchase a sleeve board. This looks like a tiny version of a regular ironing board, only you can slide a sleeve onto it to press without leaving a crease. It is also very helpful for pressing armhole seams. I even use my sleeve board for pressing bags. I find that the narrow end allows me to reach small areas to shape and press.

Pressing cloths are also a great tool. I just use a plain white flour sack towel for this. If you are pressing velveteen or any fabric with a nap, this will prevent the iron from leaving permanent marks on the fabric.

You can wad up a pressing cloth and place it inside a bag to help you shape it with pressing and steaming. The result will be a professional finish.

Use your iron and sleeve board to help manipulate unusual shapes. Here I am only pressing to crease the top portion of a bag that has a narrower opening and flares toward the bottom with rounded corners.

Sewing Advice
Making Intentional Creases

I love to press intentional creases into some of my designs. I know that this might sound crazy, but if you have gathering in a skirt or any ruffled items, it is good to press them flat. They will have a more crisp appearance and will lie flat against the body, which is much more flattering than having clothing that appears to add bulk during wear.

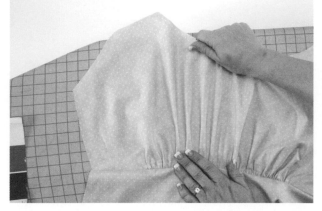

1 Lay out the piece that you want to press creases into on top of your ironing board. Fold the fabric by hand to gather it up as desired.

2 Apply a hot steam iron to the surface of the fabric, pressing in the creases. Use a pressing cloth for delicate fabrics as necessary.

Going Beyond the Basics

While I find the sleeve board and pressing cloth sufficient for my needs, your project selection may necessitate the use of other special tools. For example, if you really get into tailoring clothing, a dressmaker's ham may be something you'll want to purchase. These help shape the shoulder and other curved areas of clothing.

Embroidered Summer Skirt

FABRICS

1 precut 2½" strip roll (will use 18 total strips, so there will be leftovers)

⅛ yd. each of 4 different coordinating solid fabrics for embroidered sections

NOTIONS

Embroidery floss and needle

Fabric marking pencil such as Sewline

Polyester thread to match fabrics

Rotary cutter, ruler and mat

Small piece of fusible interfacing for reinforcing buttonholes at waist

With no pattern pieces required, this skirt is so simple to make! The design is based off of a few basic measurements, then the pieces are cut and sewn together. You will have a lovely new skirt in no time at all, and the fit is super easy and flattering with a drawstring closure.

The hand-embroidered accents on this skirt are subtly scattered throughout. It is a great illustration of how embroidery can impact the overall look of a finished skirt.

Measurements Chart

Hips	34–36"	38–50"
Yoke	¼ yd.	½ yd.
Drawstring	⅛ yd.	⅙ yd.
Hemband	⅙ yd.	⅙ yd.

Note: You can opt to make the drawstring from decorative ribbon if you choose. Purchase 2 yards of ¾" wide ribbon instead of the yardage in the chart.

The finished length of the skirt is 28".

Adjusting the Length of Your Skirt

You can adjust the length of your skirt by the width of the pieces you use, or you can manipulate the width of the hemband and make the skirt longer if you like. If you desire a shorter skirt, just use fewer pieces.

1 Measure around the fullest part of your hips and round up to the nearest even number. Refer to this hip measurement for cutting the pieces.

2 Choose 18 different fabric strips from the precut roll. Separate them into 2 groups of 9. These groups of fabrics will be alternated throughout the skirt. Because there are 8 total panels, you will cut 4 of each fabric. Decide on an order for the fabrics, putting the groups side by side the way they will be sewn so you can visualize how they will look together. Try to avoid overusing a particular color or design anywhere in the layout in order to maintain contrast.

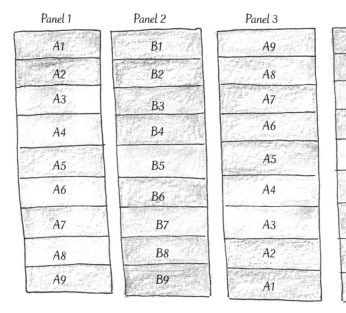

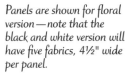

Panels are shown for floral version — note that the black and white version will have five fabrics, 4½" wide per panel.

- -- --- - **CUT THE PANEL PIECES** - --- -

1 Once you have decided on the order of the fabrics, it is time to cut them to the appropriate width. Follow the chart for your hip width and cut four pieces from each fabric. Smaller sizes will have more fabric left over. Keep the order you have chosen for each group. To keep it simple, think of one group as A and the other as B.

Hips	Panel Width
34	8"
36	8¼"
38	8½"
40	8¾"
42	9"
44	9¼"
46	9½"
48	9¾"
50	10"

2 Once the pieces have been cut, begin the layout. Lay out the first stack from Group A the way it will be sewn together, going top to bottom. Repeat with a stack from Group B. For the third panel, go back to Group A and order the fabric starting from the bottom of the skirt instead of the top. For panel four, order from the bottom from Group B, as shown.

3 Repeat this process for the remaining stacks. By alternating the order of the fabrics, you will get a nicer variety in the way the fabrics come together than if they were ordered from the top for the whole skirt.

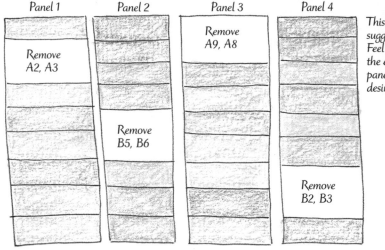

Panel 1   Panel 2   Panel 3   Panel 4

Remove A2, A3

Remove B5, B6

Remove A9, A8

Remove B2, B3

This is only a suggested layout. Feel free to place the embroidery panels where desired.

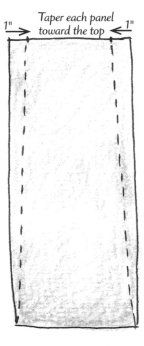

1" Taper each panel toward the top 1"

· - - · - - · CUT THE PANELS FOR EMBROIDERY · - · - - - ·

1 Cut the solid fabrics for the embroidered sections. Cut 2 pieces from each solid, 4½" long by the width specified in the chart on page 52 for your hip size. This will total 8 embroidery panels. Scatter these throughout the layout of the skirt, removing two fabric strips from each panel as shown.

2 Once all of the panels have been laid out in order, flip over the top piece on each panel to the wrong side and number them from 1–8 in the center. This is so that you can easily keep the stacks in order and know which one designates the top.

- SEW THE PANEL PIECES TOGETHER -

1 Stack up each panel in order with the numbered one on top. Stitch them right sides together with a strict ¼" seam allowance. It is very important to be as accurate as possible with the seam allowance. If you do not watch this carefully, your pieces will not match up from one panel to the next and the seams will not meet correctly.

2 Finish the edges of your seams with a machine overcast stitch if you do not have a serger. If you do have a serger, stitch the seams with it. Your machine will not trim away any fabric with a ¼" seam, so the seam allowance accuracy is pretty easy with a serger.

3 Press the seam allowances to one side. For panels 1, 3, 5 and 7, press the seam allowances toward the top of the skirt. For panels 2, 4, 6 and 8, press the seam allowances toward the bottom of the skirt. By alternating direction, it will be easier to match up the seams because they will lock against each other.

- - - - - - CUT THE PANEL WIDTH - - - - -

1 Each panel is tapered at the top, creating a subtle A-line to the skirt. To taper each panel, lay them out one at a time on your rotary mat and use a ruler to taper in from the bottom toward the top edge by 1" on both sides. Trim away the sides with the rotary cutter. Be sure that the end being tapered is the one that has the number written on the back.

2 Repeat this process for the remaining 7 panels. Once all of the panels have been tapered, lay them out in numerical order to prepare them for sewing.

- - - · SEW THE PANELS TOGETHER · - · - ·

1 Place the panels right sides together and stitch with a ½" seam allowance. Sew panels 1–4 together and then 5–8. Leave the skirt in halves to complete the hand embroidery.

2 Press the seams to one side. Choose one direction and press all seams that way, except for the large embroidered panel, which should be pressed the away from the panel.

53

- - - ADD THE HAND EMBROIDERY - - -

1   Use a fabric marking pencil to draw designs onto the fabric. For this skirt, I completed the embroidery with 3 strands of embroidery floss. I also added a running stitch in a contrasting color around the perimeter of most of the panels to make the edges look more finished. Again, do what you like!

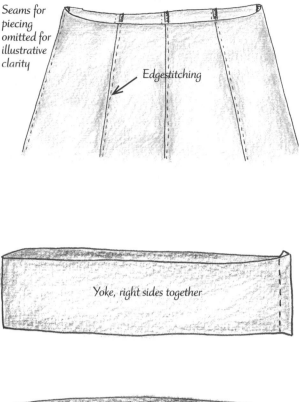

Seams for piecing omitted for illustrative clarity

Edgestitching

- - - FINISH SEWING THE MAIN SKIRT - - -

1   Once the hand embroidery is finished, press the panels thoroughly. Press your hand stitching from the wrong side or use a pressing cloth to keep from crushing any particular stitches.

2   Sew the remaining panels together in numerical order, forming a tube. Edgestitch each panel seam.

- - - - - COMPLETE THE YOKE - - - - - -

1   Yokes for all sizes are 7¾" in width. Be sure to follow the direction of the fabric print if it is directional in nature. Cut 1 or 2 of these strips from the yoke yardage as determined by your hip measurement plus 7" for ease and seam allowance.

2   If piecing of the fabric is necessary to get the correct length, place the strips right sides together along one narrow edge and stitch with a ¼" seam allowance. Press the seam to one side, then trim the piece down to the size needed.

Yoke, right sides together

3   Once the yoke piece is the correct length for your size, sew the narrow ends right sides together with a ½" seam allowance, then press the seam to one side. This should form a tube.

4   Finish the top edge of the yoke by serging or using an overcast stitch on a conventional machine. Turn the top edge toward the wrong side by 1¼" and press.

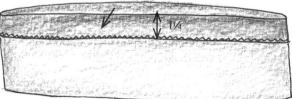

1¼"

5   For the drawstring opening, mark the center front along the top, then mark ⅛" down from there and ½" to either side for the top of the buttonholes. Mark again ¾" below the top markings for the bottom of the buttonholes. Open out the casing and add a small piece of fusible interfacing to the wrong side of the fabric behind the markings to reinforce the fabric.

½"   ½"

⅛"   ⅛"

¾"   ¾"

Top edge of yoke

6   With the casing opened out, stitch the buttonholes, then carefully cut them open. Fold the casing back down and stitch at 1" and 1¼" down from the top edge to form the casing. Edgestitch the top pressed edge.

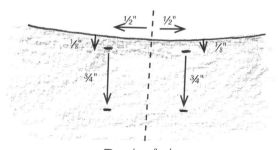

Edgestitch upper edge

Edge and topstitch lower edge of casing

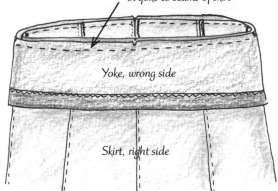

Stitch together, matching ¼" markings in yoke to seams of skirt

Yoke, wrong side

Skirt, right side

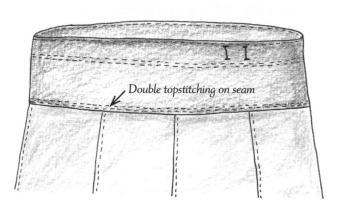

Double topstitching on seam

SEW THE YOKE AND SKIRT TOGETHER

1 Mark the lower edge of the yoke into 4 equal sections.

2 Place the yoke and skirt sections right sides together, matching up the markings with every other seam. Pin in place.

3 Stitch the yoke and skirt sections together with a ½" seam allowance. Press the seam toward the yoke, then double topstitch on the lower yoke.

CREATE THE HEMBAND

1 Cut 2 strips of fabric 3" wide by the width of the fabric. Piece them right sides together along one of the narrow ends with a ¼" seam allowance to form one long strip. Press the seam open.

2 Fold in ½" to the wrong side at one of the narrow ends and press.

3 Fold the strip in half wrong sides together so that it measures 1½" in width and press.

4 Place the pressed end of the band against the right side of the skirt at the lower edge, beginning with one of the seams that will be along the back of the skirt. Sew about 1½" in from the pressed edge and stitch all the way around until just before the beginning is reached. Allow enough extra on the band fabric to tuck inside the pressed end by about ½". Trim away any excess beyond that. Tuck the raw end inside the pressed one and finish stitching the seam.

5 Edge finish the seam by serging or overcasting with a conventional machine. Press the seam toward the skirt.

6 Double topstitch the seam along the lower edge just above the hemband seam on the skirt. Then, double topstitch along the lower finished edge of the hemband itself.

½"

Wrong side

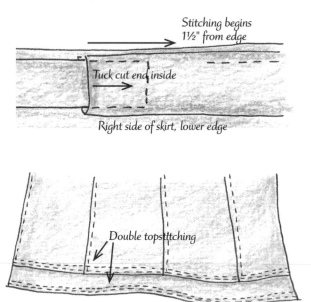

Stitching begins 1½" from edge

Tuck cut end inside

Right side of skirt, lower edge

Double topstitching

--- -- MAKE THE DRAWSTRING · --- -

You can choose to make a drawstring in the following steps or you can use some decorative ribbon instead. It's your choice!

1 Cut 2 strips 2" wide by the width of fabric for hip sizes 34–40 or 3 strips for hip sizes 42–50. Piece them right sides together along the narrow edges with a ¼" seam allowance to form one long strip. Press seam(s) open.

2 Fold the strip right sides together and stitch down the long edges with a ¼" seam allowance.

3 Using a large safety pin, turn right side out and press with the seam along one side.

4 Edgestitch both long sides of the drawstring.

5 Use the safety pin once more to insert the drawstring into one of the buttonholes on the upper edge of the yoke, and pull it all the way through to the remaining buttonhole. Pull the drawstring so that an even amount is coming out of each buttonhole.

6 Try on the skirt and pull up the drawstring until the skirt is resting on your body where you desire, then tie into a bow or knot. If there is a lot of extra length on the tails of the drawstring, trim away the undesired amount.

7 Turn up each end of the drawstring by ¼" twice, then stitch in place to finish.

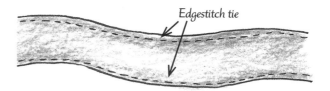

Edgestitch tie

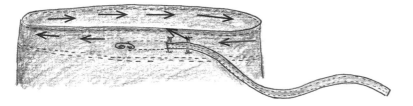

Stitch across end

--- --- -- PRESS THE SKIRT --- --- -

1 Pull up the drawstring as if you were wearing your skirt and press intentional creases into the fabric. See the technique on page 49. This will make the skirt lay in a flattering way on your body.

Express Yourself with Embroidery

Hand embroidery really does allow you to express your personality. It provides you an opportunity to use colors you like and designs that inspire you, showing the world a glimpse of the things that move you most. You may even decide to use some beads or other accents to add yet another dimension to your work. But don't fuss too much—hand embroidery has its own charm, even if you're just a beginner!

Time for Reflection

Did you learn any new embroidery stitches? If so, which are your favorites?

_____
_____
_____
_____
_____
_____
_____
_____

What else do you plan to add embroidery to?

_____
_____
_____
_____
_____
_____
_____
_____
_____

What is your favorite part about working with precut fabrics? Would you use them again in a future project? Why or why not?

_____
_____
_____
_____
_____
_____
_____
_____

Sewing Advice
Working With Color

Working with color can be challenging. There are so many factors to consider, such as the intensity of the color and the printed pattern of the fabric. These factors can make fabrics blend well with others and almost read as a solid from a distance, or they can help create bold and striking contrast within a piece.

When planning for a large project such as a quilt, it is best to gather up the fabrics you'll be using and spend some time examining them, individually and together. I like to start by sorting darks, mediums and lights into different piles and work from there. In the case of the *In the Round Picnic Quilt* project (see page 60), I did just that. I sorted the fabrics first and then planned the layout of the fabrics.

When working on a project of large scale, it is best to have a place where you can lay out the fabric and stand away from it to see how it is going to come together. This helps you see problem areas ahead of time before you begin sewing. For example, maybe there is too heavy of a concentration of one color in a particular spot, or too many fabrics of the same value clustered together. If you do spot problems with your layout, don't get discouraged. Successful fabric placement is a trial and error process, and the more you practice, the more instinctual it will become.

If you are just starting out, it can be helpful to work within one collection of fabrics. Designers typically have a few signature pieces in a collection, and the rest will be made up of coordinating fabrics that compliment these main pieces. Usually there are a few colorways, or themes in different colors. These usually blend well, and can be mixed and matched or used together for a scrappy sort of look. You also have the option of choosing your favorite colorway and working exclusively within it. By doing this, you will eliminate any stress associated with having to blend different variations of one color across different manufacturers. This is particularly helpful if all of this is new to you.

It is also important to trust your own eye when it comes to selecting a color scheme. Remember, beauty is in the eye of the beholder! There is an infinite number of combinations that can be made with different colors and fabrics. If you find yourself drawn to certain colors or patterns, it is your subconscious driving you toward your choices. Really try to hone in on your intuitions and don't be afraid to trust yourself. I find that the biggest reason people don't choose certain fabrics or combine them with others is that they are afraid to do it. The world will not come to an end if it isn't perfect. The only way to learn this skill is to practice it!

Sewing Advice
The Fabric That Binds

Binding is a useful way to finish many different edges. It can finish the edge of a quilt, the hem of a skirt or the top of a bag, just to name a few. The type of edge you are binding will determine whether or not the binding is used straight of grain or bias. For straight edges, straight of grain fabric can be used. This means you can cut across the width or along the length of the fabric to attain your strips for the binding. If the edge is curved at all, you will need to cut the strips on the bias to give them added flexibility to conform to the edge without puckering.

To create a binding, you must first decide how much of it you want to be visible from either side of the item you are adding it to. Once you have decided on the width, some simple math can be done to calculate how wide the strip will need to be cut. For example, let's say that I want to see ½" of binding on either side of the edge. Double that and I am now at 1". I personally like my bindings to be double the thickness in fabric, so I would double it again, which brings us to 2". Now I have to factor in the seam allowance. I usually keep the seam allowance on a binding to ⅜". I will need that for each raw edge, which adds ¾". In the end, it means that I will need to cut my strips 2¾" wide. This will be folded in half down the center and result in a 1⅜" wide double fabric strip. Once the seam allowance is subtracted, I will end up with ½" to either side of the edge just as I wanted!

1. Once the strips are all cut, sew them right sides together. Use a ¼" seam allowance and press the seams open. Then, fold the long unit of strips in half down the center, wrong sides together, match up the raw edges, and press it flat.

2. To prepare the project for binding, open out one end and press at least ¼" to the wrong side to finish that end. Fold the strip unit closed again and press.

3. To apply the binding, start with the finished end against the side that will not face outward. For example, this would mean the interior of a bag or the back side of a quilt. With the raw edges even, begin pinning the binding to the project. Once you have reached the finished end of the binding, leave ½" extra and trim away the rest. Open out the finished end and place the cut end inside, concealing the cut edge.

4. Stitch the binding in place with a ¼" or ⅜" seam allowance, depending on the project.

5. Once it has been stitched in place, fold the binding around the raw edge to the front so that it is concealed. Pin and press the binding in place, then edgestitch along the lower folded edge.

Simple Formula for Cutting Binding

Width desired x 2 + ¾" = Width of binding strip to cut

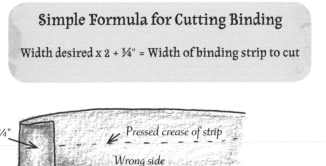

¼"

Pressed crease of strip

Wrong side

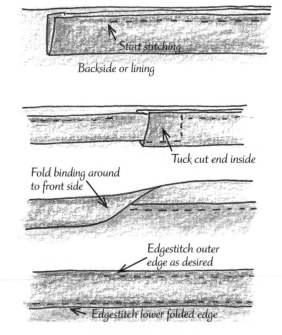

Start stitching

Backside or lining

Tuck cut end inside

Fold binding around to front side

Edgestitch outer edge as desired

Edgestitch lower folded edge

In the Round Picnic Quilt

FABRICS

68 10" squares

5 yd. fabric for backing

1 yd. binding

NOTIONS

¼" quilting foot (helpful but not required)

Approximately 80" square of batting of your choice (cotton was used in the project)

Fabric marking pencil

Flexible measuring tape

Polyester thread to match fabrics

Rotary cutter, ruler and mat

Adding the Perfect Subtle Accent

When deciding on the quilting for this project, I really took the design of the fabric into account. I wanted the fabric to be the star and the stitches of the machine quilting to be the perfect accent. Instead of using white thread, I chose a light gray, a prominent part of the color palette in my chosen fabrics. The result is subtle yet complimentary. Don't overlook the possibility of using a subtle color for your quilting!

Doesn't this picnic quilt just ooze happiness and a carefree summer attitude? I think so! It makes me want to run right out and gather up goodies to have a picnic. What a perfect wedding gift this would make along with a lovely bottle of wine and other goodies!

I have a confession to make—I am not a quilter! I do love quilts and appreciate all the work that goes into them, but most of them just take too long to make and the project suffers as a result of my short attention span. But this particular project goes so quickly that it is hard to believe you've just made a quilt! It is ideal for a beginner or for someone who wants a finished project in a hurry. The staggered blocks lend a brick sort of feel to the design, which I love for two reasons. One, I don't have to match seams, and two, I love the illusion!

For further ease, I utilized the convenience of precut 10" squares so I could get right to the layout and sewing. As I have said before, choosing fabrics can be very time consuming. When you choose to use a pack of fabric squares, a lot of the work has already been done for you. What a relief! If you do choose to use your own fabrics, be sure to read the article on working with color on page 58.

The finished quilt is 76" in diameter.

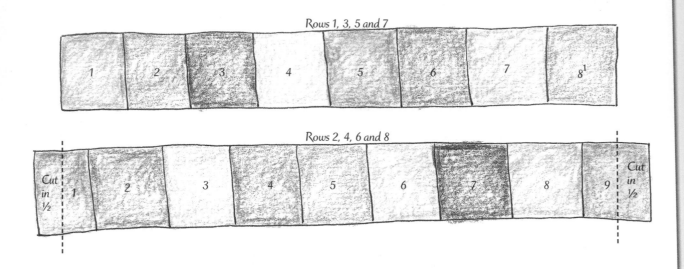

Rows 1, 3, 5 and 7

| 1 | 2 | 3 | 4 | 5 | 6 | 7 | 8^1 |

Rows 2, 4, 6 and 8

Cut in ½ | 1 | 2 | 3 | 4 | 5 | 6 | 7 | 8 | 9 | Cut in ½

- - - - - - - - PLAN THE LAYOUT - - - - - - -

1 Separate your fabrics into lights, mediums and darks. Begin the layout, one row at a time, watching that you are not clustering like patterns or color too much in any one spot.

2 The rows will alternate between 8 and 9 squares. Rows 1, 3, 5 and 7 will have 8 squares and Rows 2, 4, 6 and 8 will have 9 squares.

3 The rows with 9 squares will have the first and last square cut in half so that the seams from one row to the next will be staggered.

4 It is recommended that you lay the entire top out on a large surface like the floor to see the piece as a whole. This will enable you to see if you have too much of the same color or pattern in one spot. Make adjustments as needed, then stack up each row and number them in order.

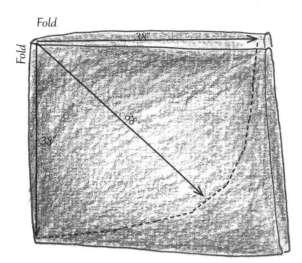

Fold

Fold

38"

38"

38"

- - - SEW THE SQUARES TOGETHER - - -

1 The seam allowances are ¼" for this project. Begin stitching each row of squares right sides together and press the seams to one side.

2 Repeat for each row until all of the rows have been sewn together, then sew each of the rows to each other, keeping them in numerical order. Press the seams to one side.

Seams from piecing omitted

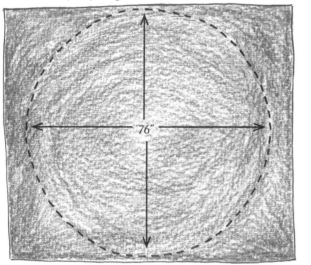

76"

- - - - - - - MARK THE QUILT - - - - - - -

1 Once the top has been sewn together, fold it into fourths with the right side facing out. Measure from the folded center out to the raw edges. This should be approximately 38".

2 Using the flexible measuring tape as your guide, begin to pivot from the center point to the edges, marking an arc for the first quarter of the quilt. Repeat this process for the remaining 3 quarters of the quilt to mark the circle.

Seam Allowances

Most quilting calls for a ¼" seam allowance to be used. This project is pretty forgiving if you aren't a perfect ¼" person like me! That said, I do have a ¼" machine foot that I use to keep me honest. All I have to do is keep the edges of the fabric lined up with the edge of the foot and stitch—it's really that simple! This way I can let my mind wander a little while I'm piecing my squares together. Who says you can't daydream while sewing?

- - - - - - PREPARE THE BACKING - - - - -

1 For the quilt backing, cut the 5 yard length of fabric into two 2½ yard lengths. Remove the selvedges from the edges, then stitch the two pieces right sides together down one of the long edges with a ½" seam allowance. Press the seam to one side.

2 Layer the pieces together and begin quilting. It is highly recommended that you leave the quilt as a rectangle for the quilting process, then cut it on the lines to make it into a circle just before binding it. This project was quilted by a professional long arm quilter on her machine. You can choose to have your project professionally quilted or quilt the project yourself using a walking foot. You could also hand tie the quilt if you like.

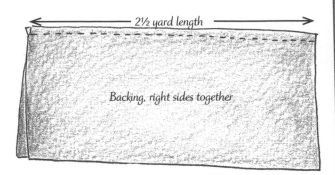

2½ yard length

Backing, right sides together

- - - - - - - - BINDING - - - - - - - -

1 Once you've finished with the quilting, cut it out on the lines to make it into a circle.

2 Following the technique detailed on page 29, cut a series of 3" strips on the bias for the binding. You will need about 6½ yards' worth to make it all the way around.

3 Read the article on binding on page 59 to add the binding to the quilt using a ⅜" seam allowance.

4 Machine edgestitch the binding in place, then edgestitch again near the outer folded edge.

Ideas for Adapting This Project

Use fewer squares and make a smaller circular quilt for a baby's playmat.

Make it larger and use it as an area rug. It washes beautifully and you can even treat it with Scotchgard to keep it clean during use!

Use 5" squares and make mini versions as chargers for dinner plates.

Time for Reflection

If this was your first time to make a quilt top, what did you think of the process? What part was your favorite?

_____

_____

_____

_____

_____

_____

_____

What would you do differently next time?

_____

_____

_____

_____

_____

_____

_____

_____

_____

If you used precut squares, what did you find to be most helpful about using them? Would you consider using them for other projects?

_____

_____

_____

_____

_____

_____

_____

_____

_____

NOTES

NOTES

Chapter Three
AUTUMN

Fall is undoubtedly a magical time of year. Who can deny the splendor of leaves changing color and swirling about in a cool, crisp breeze, or the glorious smells and tastes of a bountiful autumn harvest? School starts once again, too, and everyone is ready for a fresh start and new things to learn.

This chapter features all you could ever want to know about stabilizers, making the perfect handle for all of your bag projects, working with laminates and quilting your own fabric. You'll use these pointers to craft two projects perfect for the back-to-school season—a notebook satchel and an insulated lunch bag. The satchel is a great way to carry your spiral notebook in style while keeping your writing tools and other important items organized. Likewise, the insulated bag makes the perfect lunchtime accessory and it's friendly to the environment! So, without further ado, let's get this class started!

Autumn Sewing Goals

This fall, I will:

_____

_____

_____

_____

Classes I want to take:

_____

_____

_____

_____

Techniques I want to master:

_____

_____

_____

_____

Projects I intend to sew:

_____

_____

_____

_____

_____

_____

AUTUMN CHECKLIST

Items I need to purchase for my projects:

_____

_____

_____

_____

Gifts to Sew This Season

Item:

For: on the occasion of

Started:

Notions needed:

Materials needed:

Notes:

Item:

For: on the occasion of

Started:

Notions needed:

Materials needed:

Notes:

Item:

For: on the occasion of

Started:

Notions needed:

Materials needed:

Notes:

Item:

For: on the occasion of

Started:

Notions needed:

Materials needed:

Notes:

A Firm Foundation: Working With Stabilizers

It seems there are about a million different stabilizers in the marketplace today. You may be asking yourself "Why do we need so many kinds, and what are they all used for?" Aren't they all the same? In a word, no! Stabilizers are fascinating things, but knowing which kind to use when will determine whether your finished project is a rousing success or a dismal failure.

Because there is so much confusion when it comes to stabilizers, a great number of stitchers often use the wrong one or none at all. This is truly unfortunate, as the right stabilizer can do so much for your projects. However, taking just a few minutes to educate yourself on stabilizers can help you avoid those unforeseen sewing disasters.

Let's start with the *why*. When I started sewing as a girl, my mother advised that I use some sort of stabilizer any time that the pattern required it. I thought this seemed like an extra step that shouldn't really matter until my mother explained it to me. Her basic message for me was this: A stabilizer provides extra structure to a project in key areas and, if I leave it out, I would regret it. Well, my mother was right as usual! But, of course, my impatience led to omitting the stabilizer a few times early on in my sewing life, forcing me to learn the hard way. Aren't those always the lessons that stick with us best? Please, allow me to spare you that pain—learn vicariously through me on this one!

Think of stabilizer like the bones in your body or the framing of a house. Sure, you could have some sort of body or home without those things, but it wouldn't last very long. Stabilizer does the exact same thing for anything you sew, and when a pattern requires it, it is best to stick with the plan. After all, the designer had a specific outcome in mind, and I guarantee that you won't achieve that same result if you omit it.

The same can be said for thinking that stabilizers are all the same. They are not. There are numerous thicknesses, degrees of stiffness and so on. Unless you are quite familiar with how one product stacks up against another, it is best to find what the pattern specifically calls for. When you substitute with a different product, you may unknowingly be causing more trouble for yourself when you attempt to sew the project together. If the stabilizer is thicker and stiffer than what was called for, you might find that the sewing is next to impossible. On the other hand, if something much lighter weight is used, then the project may be floppy with no backbone at all.

I developed the handy chart on the next page to illustrate the differences between stabilizers. These are the kinds I use most, and they are readily available just about anywhere. Most local fabric stores should have them, but if you have trouble finding them, you can always go online. I try not to use anything obscure in my work, but I do realize that products differ from one country to another, which can complicate things a bit. If you live outside the U.S., hopefully you can find these products online or your local shopkeeper can recommend a suitable substitute.

Stabilizer	Width	Fusible?	Uses:
Pellon 911FF	20"	Yes	This is my "go-to" stabilizer. It is very versatile and is perfect for the facings of a skirt or dress, the lining of a bag and the interlining of handles. It is easy to sew through and holds up well to washing and use.
Pellon Peltex 71F	20"	Yes	This is a heavy weight stabilizer that is fusible on one side and perfect for making a project that needs some serious structure. I use it a lot for the outer structure of bags. It is also nice for placing in the bottom of a bag during construction as it provides extra strength so the bag doesn't get saggy.
Pellon Fusible Thermolam Plus TP971F	45"	Yes	This is a polyester fleece product that is fusible on one side. This is much softer than Peltex and as a result will not provide the same kind of structure. It is great to use in placemats and soft bags and looks nice when machine quilted. It holds up very well to machine washing and drying.
Sulky KK#2000 or 505	N/A	No	This is a temporary spray adhesive. It is great to use when you need to stick a few things together just long enough to stitch them, and it dissipates in a day or two so it doesn't have to be washed out. I like to use it with stabilizers that are not otherwise fusible. It works well in cases where pinning is not practical, like when working with laminates or stiff stabilizers. I often use it instead of pinning a paper pattern to Peltex.
Roc-Lon Multi-Purpose Cloth	54"	No	This is a fairly new stabilizer for me. It is very much like a canvas and some people know it as "blackout" for blocking light at windows. It is very flexible and lightweight, but still has a lot of body. It is easy to sew through and holds up well.
The Warm Company Insul-Bright	22.5"	No	This is a product that is perfect for creating an insulated bag. It has a foil material that is sandwiched inside a fleece-like fiber that creates the insulating quality. I love it for oven mitts, hot pads and insulated bags. It has soft body and lends a nice loft for machine quilting.
Pellon Shape-Flex	20"	Yes	Shape-Flex is a woven stabilizer with fusible product on one side. It is the woven counterpart to the 911FF product listed earlier. It is great to add to the back of panels that you are planning to hand embroider. It adds a small amount of body without being bulky. I like to add it to light-colored fabrics before embroidering since it makes the fabric less transparent thus making my thread carries on the back of my work disappear!

Sewing Advice
Handling the Situation

Handles are such an important part of a project. If not made properly, they will wear out long before the rest of the project does. There is a simple foolproof way that I have been making handles for years. They stand up well to heavy use and continue to look good throughout the life of the item during its use.

There are a couple of key issues surrounding handles. One is how they are made and the other is how they are attached to the project. I can't tell you how many bag patterns I see where the handle has been incorporated into the seam along the top of the bag. This is the first place that a bag will begin to tear if overloaded. Sometimes a repair can be made, but a lot of times the fabric will rip and it will take some creativity to fix it.

This can be easily remedied if the handle is attached in a different manner. For most of my designs, the handles extend the full length of the bag all the way to the bottom. This gives you the entire side of the bag to stitch the handle to, thus distributing the weight and burden that the handles have to take every time the bag is carried. Your odds of the handle staying in excellent condition (not to mention the rest of the bag) are greatly increased.

Another manner in which handles can be better incorporated into a design is to have some sort of hardware involved. This may mean that there are ring tabs sewn somewhere to the bag and then the handle is attached to that hardware. This is a good sturdy way to attach a handle since most of the time, the ring tab is being sewn through the entire side of the bag exterior to attach it. By backstitching and sewing a couple of lines of stitching, you ensure that the tab will stay in place to support the handle that is attached to it.

Most any pattern can be modified to accommodate such changes. To add handles that run the height of the bag, they would need to be made longer and attached before the bag is sewn, but with a bit of careful planning, this can be accomplished. This method requires more fabric for the handle, so purchasing a bit extra if you are planning on changing some handles is probably a good idea. The hardware method is easier to implement and shouldn't use much more fabric than a pattern originally calls for.

My favorite way to make handles is by sewing two interfaced strips together with a good ½" seam allowance. I leave the seam allowance fully intact, fold in the outer edges, and then fold the whole thing closed before stitching. This gives you the thickness of several layers of fabric without being too much to sew through.

Check out my favorite technique for making handles on the following page. The Notebook Satchel and Insulated Lunch Bag projects in this chapter both use this type of handle.

Sewing Advice

Making Handles

1 Place two strips right sides together and stitch down one of the long sides with a ½" seam allowance. Press the seam open.

2 Fold in one of the outer raw edges so that it just touches the raw edge of the seam allowance and press.

3 Repeat for the other outer raw edge.

4 Fold the handle strip in half along the seam, with wrong sides together, and press.

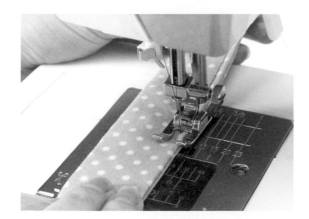

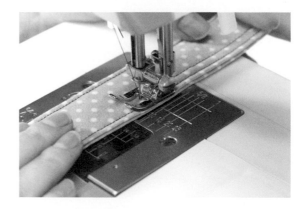

5 Edgestitch down the long open side of the handle, then down the long finished edge. To edgestitch, begin at one end and follow the finished edge all the way around a piece. I like to stay within ¹⁄₁₆" to ⅛" away from the edge for this stitching.

6 Topstitch each side. To topstitch, begin again at the same end where the edgestitching started, only this time, complete the stitching approximately ¼" in from the previous stitching line. Notice how I use the outer edge of my machine foot to gauge the distance evenly all the way around the piece.

Repeat for any remaining handle strips, then trim the handles down to the length specified in the instructions.

Autumn Sewing Project
Notebook Satchel

FABRICS

⅓ yd. Fabric A for main exterior and small interior pocket

⅓ yd. Fabric B for contrast exterior and main interior

¼ yd. Fabric C for tab and handles

⅓ yd. Fabric D for large interior pockets

⅓ yd. Fabric E for bias binding

STABILIZERS

⅔ yd. Pellon Peltex 71

1 yd. Pellon 911FF lightweight fusible interfacing

NOTIONS

¾" magnetic snap

9" vinyl sport zipper

Fabric marking pencil such as Sewline

Polyester thread to match fabrics

Rotary cutter, ruler and mat

Zipper foot

Zipper pull (optional)

What better way to get ready for the start of a new school year than with this cute notebook satchel? This clever project lets you carry your sketchbook or spiral notebook in style! With an outside pocket for stashing pens, pencils and your phone, this bag is great for both adults and children alike. The inside also features a small pocket and another handy spot to stash a pen or pencil, keeping those essential items right at your fingertips. The magnetic tab closure and handles make this satchel easy to grab and go!

Alternative Hardware

I love the magnetic snap for this satchel, but if you want to mix things up a little, you can always add a twist lock instead. These locks are installed in a similar manner, and adding one to your bag will give it a touch of metallic shine. See the Resources list on page 124 for where to purchase the hardware.

The finished bag is 10½" wide x 12¼" tall x 1" deep. It can accommodate up to a 150-page spiral bound notebook with exterior dimensions of 11" x 9".

- - - - - - MAKE THE EXTERIOR - - - - - - -

1 Cut a 12" × 22" piece of Peltex, very slightly rounding each corner.

2 Cut an 18" × 12" rectangle from Fabric A, with the fabric direction following the 12" width. Cut a 5" × 12" piece from Fabric B. Pin the two right sides together with Fabric B on the right hand end. Stitch together with a ½" seam allowance.

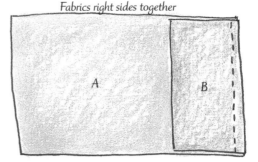

Fabrics right sides together

3 Press the seam open, then place the fabric unit right side facing up on top of the fusible side of the Peltex with edges even. Iron in place, then trim the corners of the fabric to match the Peltex. Edgestitch to either side of the contrast fabric seam.

4 Add one half of the magnetic snap (the receiving side) to the satchel exterior on the contrast fabric, ¾" in from the edge and centered top to bottom. Mark, then snip two small holes for the prongs. Install the snap and reinforcement plate, and bend prongs outward on the wrong side.

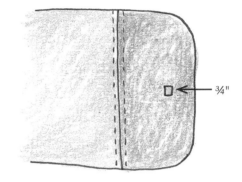

- - - ADD THE LINING AND ZIPPER - - -

1 Cut a 12" × 22" rectangle from Fabric B. On the wrong side of the fabric, Measure down 3½" from one of the 12" ends and mark a line. Mark another line 3" from the edge, then mark 1½" in from each side to create a skinny rectangle approximately 9" × ½" in size. This will be the opening for the inset zipper.

2 Place the lining fabric on top of the exterior, right sides together, with the zipper opening marking on top of the contrast fabric of the exterior. Pin in place around the marking with the raw edges even.

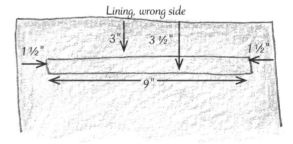

Lining, wrong side

3 Following steps 5–7 on page 17, complete the installation of the zipper.

4 Complete two lines of stitching around the zipper opening. From the wrong side, trim away the excess zipper tape beyond the stitching lines.

5 Pin the outside edges of the lining to the exterior so that they are even, then trim the corners of the lining fabric to be even with the Peltex. Stitch a scant ¼" in from the edges to hold all layers together.

6 On the exterior side, measure in 10½" and 11½" from one of the narrow ends and draw a line at each marking. Stitch down the markings, then fold and press to crease. This forms the spine of the satchel.

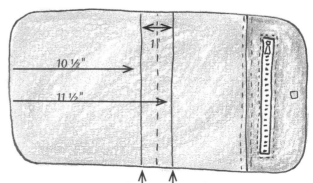

Stitch down these markings

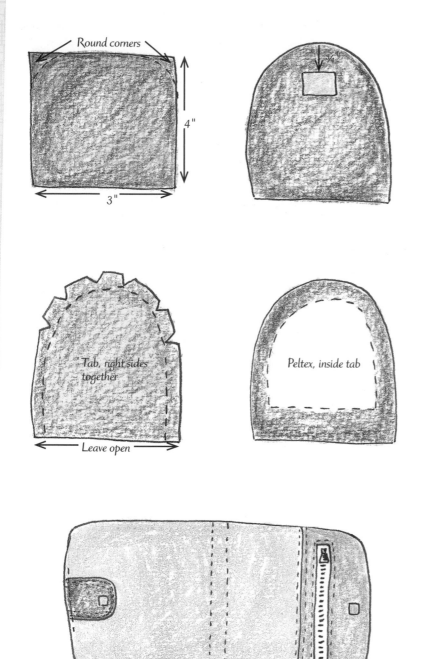

Round corners

4"

3"

¾"

Tab, right sides together

Leave open

Peltex, inside tab

MAKE THE TAB CLOSURE

1   For the tab closure, cut two 3"
    × 4" rectangles from Fabric C as
    well as the interfacing. Fuse the
    interfacing to the wrong side of
    the fabric. Slightly round two of
    the corners at one of the 3" ends.

2   Add the remaining half of the
    magnetic snap to one of the tabs
    on the right side of the fabric at
    the rounded end. Measure in ¾"
    from one of the rounded 3" ends
    and center side to side. Mark and
    snip for the prongs, then install
    the snap.

3   Place the remaining half of the
    tab on top, right sides together,
    and stitch along 3 of the sides,
    leaving the straight 3" end open.
    Wedge clip the curves, then turn
    right side out and press.

4   Cut a 2" × 3" piece of Peltex and
    round 2 of the corners slightly
    at one of the 2" ends. Slip the
    Peltex into the tab all the way
    down to the finished seam, then
    press in place. Double topstitch
    the finished edges of the tab.

5   Add the tab to the exterior of
    the satchel, centered on the 12"
    end with the snap side facing up.
    Stitch across the end, a scant ¼"
    in from the raw edges.

- - - - - - - ADD THE HANDLES - - - - - - -

1 For the handles, cut four 3" × 12" strips from Fabric C and the interfacing. Fuse the interfacing to the wrong side of the fabric.

2 Make the handles following the steps in the article on page 75.

3 Once the handles are complete, lay them out and measure 2" in from each end, then mark. Fold the handles in half and stitch between the markings.

4 On the satchel exterior, mark 3" in from each end along the 12" sides. Center each handle on this marking, with the handle lying against the exterior of the satchel folded side up. Stitch across the ends, a scant ¼" in from the edges.

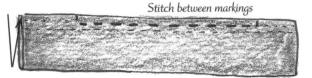

Stitch between markings

- - - - - - COMPLETE THE LARGE INTERIOR POCKETS - - - - -

1 For the large pocket on the interior left, cut a 12" × 21" rectangle from Fabric D and the interfacing. Fuse the interfacing to the wrong side of the fabric.

2 Fold the pocket piece in half wrong sides together so that it measures 12" × 10½" and press.

3 To add the small pocket, cut a 7½" × 8½" rectangle from Fabric A and the interfacing. The direction of the fabric should run parallel with the 8½" length. Fuse the interfacing to the wrong side of the fabric.

4 Fold the rectangle in half right sides together so that it measures 7½" × 4¼". Stitch around the outside edges with a ¼" seam allowance and leave an opening for turning.

5 Clip the corners diagonally, then turn right side out and press. Turn the opening edges to the inside along the seam allowance and press. Double topstitch the top folded edge.

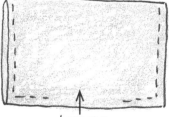

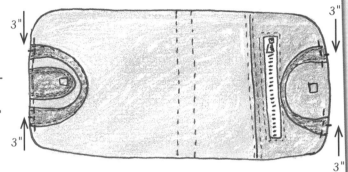

Pocket, right sides together

Leave open

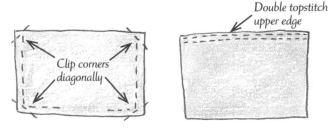

Clip corners diagonally

Double topstitch upper edge

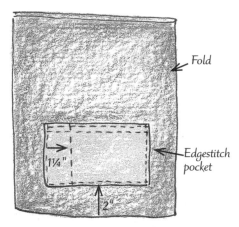

Fold

Edgestitch
pocket

1¼"

2"

6 Add the pocket to the large interior pocket, 2" up from the lower 10½" edge and centered side to side. Pin, then edgestitch in place. Measure in 1¼" from the left side of the pocket and mark. Stitch down the marking to create a holder for a pen or pencil.

7 Add the large interior pocket to the lining along the left side (this is the zippered side) with the small pocket facing up. The edges should be even and the fold of the large pocket should be just to the inside of the spine stitching. Pin in place, then trim the corners to be even with the rest of the satchel. Stitch together, a scant ¼" in from the edges, then double topstitch the folded edge of the large pocket through all thicknesses.

8 For the remaining large interior pocket, cut a 12" × 18" rectangle from Fabric D and the interfacing. Fuse the interfacing to the wrong side of the fabric, then fold the pocket piece in half wrong sides together so that it measures 12" × 9" and press. Double topstitch the folded edge of the large pocket.

9 Place the pocket on the right hand side of the lining with edges even and the folded edge 1½" in from the spine stitching. Pin in place and round the corners of the pocket. Stitch a scant ¼" in from all outer edges, leaving the folded edge open. This is where the spiral notebook will slide into place.

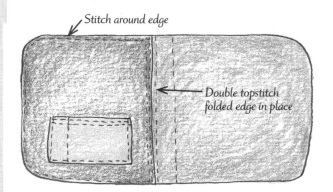

Stitch around edge

Double topstitch
folded edge in place

Stitch around outside
edges ONLY to
attach

Leave free

- ATTACH THE BINDING -

1 For the binding, cut six 3" wide strips on the bias from Fabric E. Refer to the article on page 29 to piece the strips and for pressing instructions.

2 To add the binding to the satchel, follow the binding instructions on page 59.

3 Edgestitch the folded edge of the binding in place, then edgestitch the outer finished edge.

4 Fold the handles and tab out away from the satchel and stitch across the lower edges of those pieces. Stitch again along the tab and handles in line with the outer edgestitching to reinforce.

5 Fold the tab around to connect with the snap half on the front of the satchel and crease the tab where it folds around to the front roughly 2½" in from the rounded end and mark. Stitch across the tab to crease. Attach the zipper pull to the zipper as desired.

6 Install the spiral notebook and other supplies and enjoy!

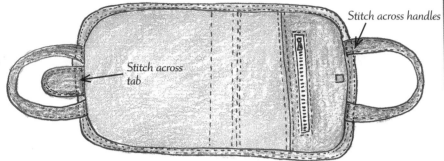

Stitch across handles

Stitch across tab

2½"

Stitch across tab, then fold and press along stitching and crease

Time for Reflection

What did you like best about this project?

_____
_____
_____
_____
_____
_____
_____
_____

How do you feel about your fabric selection? Would you change anything if you could? If so, what?

_____
_____
_____
_____
_____
_____
_____
_____
_____

What other projects would you like to add these types of handles to?

_____
_____
_____
_____
_____
_____
_____
_____

A Lofty Idea: Quilting Your Own Fabric

Quilting your own fabric is surprisingly easy and requires only a touch of patience and planning. Of course, a good walking foot for your machine doesn't hurt either!

You may be wondering how learning such a skill could come in handy for your projects. One of the many advantages to quilting your fabric is that it helps keep layers in place. More specifically, if you are working with a stabilizer that is not fusible, but you want the layers to remain together as the project is being used, quilting the fabric works great. By simply layering the fabric with the stabilizer and adding a few lines of quilting, you can ensure that the layers of your project remain intact just as you intended.

The extra stitching quilting offers can also bring a new dimension and added texture to the look of a project. I particularly like to do this with bags. All you need to achieve this look is the fabric you'll be quilting, a stabilizer, some thread, and a walking foot for your machine. I often get asked about the walking foot. While I like using a walking foot for a number of reasons, I find the most important reason to be this: I like my fabric to be evenly distributed across the stabilizer and I don't care for puckers! The walking foot allows layers to evenly feed through the machine so that you always get a nice smooth result.

To get started, I like to cut whatever stabilizer I am using to the size I need for the project. I then spray it with a temporary adhesive like Sulky KK#2000 or 505 (see the stabilizer chart on page 73 for more info), and place the fabric on top, right side up. After a bit of smoothing with my hands, it is ready to stitch.

You can stitch quilting any way you like. You can keep it simple and just do horizontal or vertical lines, or you can go diagonally. I usually aim to keep my stitching lines roughly 2½" to 3" apart. You can do any combination of these to create a grid or cross-hatch pattern. You could even follow the pattern in the fabric to make the stitching more interesting. The main purpose here is to hold the layers together. It can be as simple or complex as you desire.

Once the quilting is complete, it is usually a good idea to check the size of the piece before going forward. Sometimes a piece will distort or grow, maybe even shrink. At any rate, you may need to neaten it up before going on with the project.

Examples of quilting lines on handbags

A Slippery Situation: Working with Laminates

Working with laminated fabrics often intimidates new sewers, but it doesn't have to. A little knowledge goes a long way to being successful! The biggest problem most people have with these fabrics is that the laminated side wants to stick to the bottom of their machine foot and not feed evenly through the machine. I personally find that using a walking foot is the best way to handle stitching on the laminated side. Some people like to use a Teflon foot, which is specifically made to work with various vinyls and plastics, but after I tried the walking foot, I greatly preferred it to the Teflon-coated one.

Once you catch on to this trick, working with laminates is a snap! There are a few other tips that you might find helpful:

✧ Instead of trying to pin pattern pieces to laminate, use temporary adhesive spray.

✧ Topstitch seams since they do not want to lie flat on their own.

✧ Iron the laminate gently from the back and be sparing about it. Never iron it from the front or you will melt it!

✧ It is advisable to wash a scrap and see how it does before washing a project that uses a laminate. Laminate products vary and some may delaminate. It may turn out that you will only be able to wipe the fabric clean.

✧ When working with a laminate on a piece such as a collar or pocket, make one side from plain cotton and the other from laminate, or it will be very difficult to turn right side out and get the points nice and smooth.

What if you want to make your own laminate? You can! HeatnBond makes an iron-on vinyl that can be added to any cotton. It is easy to apply and wears reasonably well. It will not be as supple as the laminate available by the yard, but if you have your heart set on a fabric that is not available as a laminate, there is a way to make it.

Laminates are now readily available at most local fabric shops. They are wonderful for many projects like raincoats, umbrellas, reusable grocery bags, lunch bags, beach bags and more. It would even make a great addition to the back of the picnic quilt project featured in chapter 2 of this book. Then you would have no worries about your quilt getting wet from the damp ground beneath!

Insulated Lunch Bag

This little bag is my own version of the little brown bag. Of course, it is far from brown and the added details of a nice closure, handle and a laminate lining make it the last lunch bag you will ever need to use! To make it even better, there is a double lining of insulated batting so you can keep your food cool while looking stylish.

FABRICS

¼ yd. Fabric A for upper exterior

¼ yd. Fabric B for lower exterior and binding

⅙ yd. Fabric C for flap and handle

½ yd. Fabric D for laminate lining

STABILIZERS

1⅝ yd. Insul-Bright

¼ yd. Pellon 911FF interfacing

⅛ yd. Pellon Peltex 71F for bag bottom reinforcement

Sulky KK#2000 or 505 temporary adhesive spray

*If you are making your own laminated fabric, purchase 1 yd. of HeatnBond iron-on vinyl

NOTIONS

⅓ yd. of ¾" wide hook and loop tape

1" D-rings × 2

Fabric marking pencil such as Sewline

Polyester thread to match fabrics

Rotary cutter, ruler and mat

Walking foot (optional, but nice for the quilting of the fabrics)

Getting a Proper Handle on Things

The handle for this bag is attached so that it runs diagonally across the top. With the addition of hardware, this handle slips perfectly to the side when you open the bag to get your food. When stitching, pay close attention to the instructions on attaching the tabs to ensure your handle is attached properly!

The finished bag is 11" tall x 8" wide x 4½" deep.

--- BEGIN SEWING THE EXTERIOR --- -

1 Cut two 8½" × 14" rectangles from Fabric A and two 6½" × 14" rectangles from Fabric B, with the direction of the print following the smaller measurements.

2 Arrange the fabrics so that Fabric A is on top and B is on the bottom. With right sides together, stitch A to B along the 14" width with a ½" seam allowance, then press the seam open.

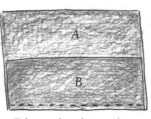

Fabrics right sides together

3 Cut two 14" squares from the Insul-Bright. Lightly spray one side of the stabilizer with temporary adhesive spray. Lay the fabric units completed in steps 1 and 2 on top of each square, with the right side of the fabric facing up and raw edges even.

4 Smooth out the fabric, then quilt the two layers together. Refer to the article on page 84 for ideas on how to quilt the fabric.

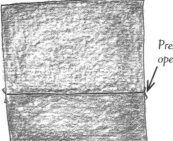

Press seam open

5 Once the quilting is complete, measure and mark 2¾" in from the sides and bottom of each bag side.

6 Add a 7" long piece of hook and loop tape to one of the bag pieces, 1" down from the top edge and centered side to side between the markings.

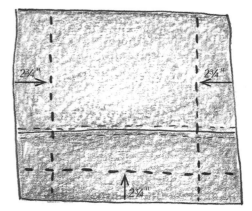

88

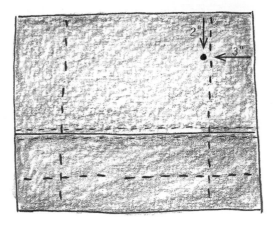

ADD THE RING TABS
AND PREPARE THE HANDLE

1 On the right hand side of each exterior piece, mark 2" down and 3" in from the corner and mark for ring tab placement.

2 Cut a 2" strip from Fabric C and 2 strips from the interfacing. Trim the selvedges from the fabric strip, then cut the strip in half. Fuse the interfacing to the wrong side of each handle piece.

3 Refer to the article on page 75 to create the handle unit.

4 Once the handle has been made, cut two 3" lengths from it for the ring tabs. Reserve the rest of the handle, which will be attached at the end of construction.

5 Place each ring tab through one of the D-rings and fold in half. Stitch across the ends ¼" from the edge.

6 Open out the tab and position the seam along one side of the loop. Place the D-ring unit onto the bag exterior piece with the seam side of the tab against the right side of the bag to conceal it. The top right corner of the tab should be resting against the marking completed in step 1, with the ring extending above the marking. Edgestitch the tab in place along the lower edge and sides, then stitch closely to the ring, being careful not to break the needle.

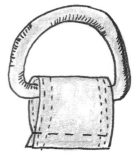

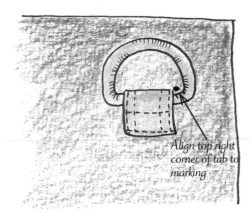

Align top right corner of tab to marking

- - - - · COMPLETE THE EXTERIOR · - - - -

1 Place the two exterior pieces right sides together and stitch with a ½" seam allowance along the sides and bottom. Measure 2¼" in from each bottom corner, including the seam allowance in the measurement, and mark.

2 Cut away each corner on the marking, then trim down the seam allowance.

3 To form the corner, open out each bottom opening and bring the side and bottom seam together. Stitch across using a ½" seam allowance, then trim the seam to ¼".

4 Turn the bag right side out and press the seams. Fold the bag along the 2¾" markings to shape the bag. Then, lay the bag flat and fold in the seams at the sides to further shape the bag. Lightly press the bag in this position to hold the shape.

5 Cut an 8" × 4½" piece of Peltex. Place it inside the bag on the bottom with the fusible side toward the Insul-Bright. From the outside of the bag (same position as when the sides were folded in for shaping), press the bag along the bottom so that the heat and steam of the iron fuse the Peltex into place.

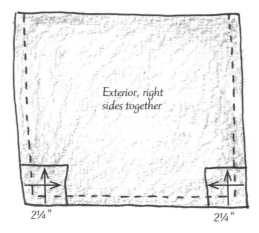

Exterior, right sides together

2¼"   2¼"

Cut away corners, then trim down seam allowance

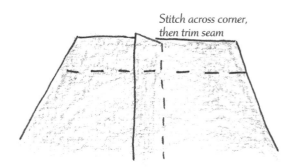

Stitch across corner, then trim seam

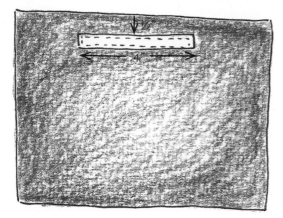

CREATE THE INTERIOR

1 Cut two 14" squares from Fabric D and the Insul-bright. If the fabric is already laminated, layer it on top of the stabilizer. If not, add the iron-on vinyl following the manufacturer's instructions.

2 Complete step 4 from Begin Sewing the Exterior. Refer to the article on page 85 for helpful tips.

3 Add a 4" strip of hook and loop tape to the top edge of each interior piece, ½" down from the top edge and centered side to side.

4 Stitch the two halves of the interior together using a ⅝" seam allowance (see steps 1–4, Complete the Exterior). This makes the interior slightly smaller than the exterior, making them fit together more easily when sewn together. Once the interior is complete, place it wrong side out inside the exterior. This should result in the two halves being wrong sides together. Smooth the interior until it fits nicely inside the exterior with the top raw edges even. Match up the side seams and pin the upper edges together. Stitch through all thicknesses, ¼" from the raw edges.

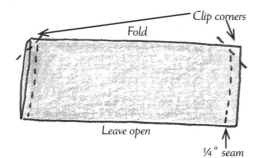

ADD THE FLAP AND BINDING

1 For the flap, cut a 6" × 8½" piece from Fabric C. Fold it in half right sides together so that it measures 3" × 8½". Stitch the narrow sides with a ¼" seam, then trim the corners diagonally. Turn right side out and press.

2 Cut a 2" × 7½" piece from the Peltex and slip inside the flap piece, getting it as close as possible to the folded edge. Press in place.

3 Add the remaining 7" piece of hook and loop tape to one side of the flap, ¼" in from the folded edge and centered. Edgestitch around the entire edge of the flap.

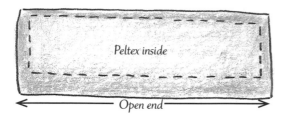

4   Add the flap to the bag against the interior, with the hook and loop tape side of the flap against the interior. This should be positioned so that the flap is resting against the half of the exterior that does not have hook and loop tape sewn to the outside.

5   With raw edges even and the flap centered on one side, stitch ¼" from the raw edge to attach.

6   For the binding, cut one strip from Fabric B, 2" wide by the width of fabric. Trim off the selvedges, then fold in one narrow end to the wrong side by ½" and press. Fold the entire strip in half widthwise, wrong sides together and press.

7   Add the binding to the bag as detailed in the article on page 59. Keep the flap against the interior until the binding is complete. Once the binding has been attached, edgestitch both finished edges.

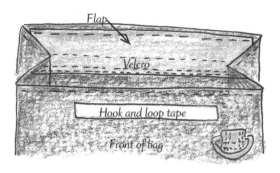

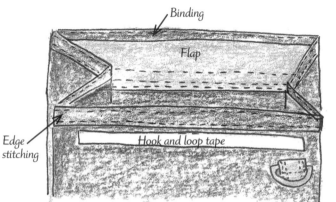

- - - - - - **ATTACH THE HANDLE** - - - - - -

1   Add the handle to the bag by placing the ends through the D-rings and folding up the raw edge by ¼" to conceal it. Stitch in place, completing 2 rows of stitching to reinforce the attachment.

To use the bag, open out the flap and bring it around to the front so it connects with the hook and loop tape on the front exterior. The hook and loop tape on the interior will hold the bag closed to hold the shape and provide an additional seal.

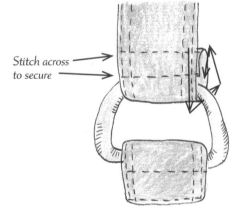

Time for Reflection

What are your thoughts on working with laminates? Would you use this type of fabric again?

_____
_____
_____
_____
_____
_____
_____

What did you learn about quilting your own fabric? Can you think of other projects where you could do this to create a special look?

_____
_____
_____
_____
_____
_____
_____
_____

Are there any adaptations you would make to this project if you had to do it over again?

_____
_____
_____
_____
_____
_____
_____
_____
_____

NOTES

NOTES

Chapter Four
WINTER

Winter—the perfect time for bundling up or snuggling near the fire. Once again, nature provides us with a lovely change of scenery. And, though the winter landscape may be stark, it's still stunning. Just picture it: Powder fresh snow blanketing the earth, creating the perfect contrast to bright red berries and lovely evergreens. With a backdrop as beautiful as this, you're bound to be inspired! Not to mention, the slow rhythm of winter is a great time for self-reflection and preparation, providing you with ample time to gear up for another year of sewing projects.

In this chapter, you will find articles on working with polar fleece, making fabric flowers, working with different closures, and caring for your sewing machine. Having these handy tricks and tips in your arsenal will help you create the most wondrous winter creations, including scarves and earwarmers like the ones featured in this chapter. When you can look this stylish, who wouldn't welcome the cold weather?

Winter Sewing Goals

This winter, I will:

_____
_____
_____
_____

Classes I want to take:

_____
_____
_____
_____
_____

Techniques I want to master:

_____
_____
_____
_____
_____

Projects I intend to sew:

_____
_____
_____
_____
_____
_____
_____
_____

WINTER CHECKLIST

Items I need to purchase for my projects:

_____
_____
_____
_____

Gifts to Sew This Season

Item:

For: on the occasion of

Started:

Notions needed:

Materials needed:

Notes:

Item:

For: on the occasion of

Started:

Notions needed:

Materials needed:

Notes:

Item:

For: on the occasion of

Started:

Notions needed:

Materials needed:

Notes:

Item:

For: on the occasion of

Started:

Notions needed:

Materials needed:

Notes:

Sewing Advice
How to Handle Polar Fleece

Polar fleece is a popular fabric. Every year it seems there are more colors and patterns to choose from. A majority is sold to make blankets and other items to keep warm in the winter, but don't let that limit your imagination. This fabric can be used for so many projects and lends itself to a lot of creativity.

If you're not familiar with polar fleece, it's certainly worth your time to learn more about this widely admired fabric and its many positive qualities. For starters, the edges do not fray when it is cut, so there is no need to worry about finishing them. Likewise, it is very easy to take care of. It can easily go from the washer to the dryer without a problem. Yet another great attribute of polar fleece is the 60" width of the fabric. Because it is so wide, it goes a long way, which means that a small project requires very little fabric. Equally important is the feel of the fabric. Polar fleece is magnificently soft and warm, and it feels great against your skin, especially for those with sensitivities to natural fabrics. In particular, it makes a great alternative for those with wool allergies, as the fabric is purely synthetic. And did I mention how affordable it is?

If you've handled polar fleece before, you might be wondering what's up with the stretch. This fabric does have a bit of stretch along the width. This is important to remember in the event that you are making something where you need to utilize this ease in the fabric. For example, a sleeve would feel more comfortable made with the stretch going across the width rather than the length. By cutting it this way, you can take advantage of the extra give of the fabric during wear. In the instance of making a blanket with the tied fringe that you see so often, it is important *not* to cut the fringe along the edges with the stretch or your fringe will be distorted. This is why you see these types of projects fringed on only two sides—the nonstretchy ones.

But how do you handle this stretch when sewing? Well, this is an easy one. Don't be intimidated by the stretch of polar fleece. It is actually quite easy to work with. Instead of a straight stitch, use a narrow but long zigzag stitch. This type of stitch has a bit of give that works well with the stretch of the fabric. Because this fabric has quite a bit of loft, no one will ever know that you didn't use a straight stitch for the sewing, since the stitches sort of hide in the fabric anyway! On my machine, I set the width of my zigzag to 2.8 and the length to 1.1, and it works beautifully. I haven't encountered any skipped stitches using a regular needle, but if you do, switch over to a needle for stretch fabrics and your problem should be solved.

Can you iron this stuff? Yes! Polar fleece can be ironed, even though you may have heard otherwise. It is best to use low heat and low steam and proceed carefully. It is true that high heat can damage the lofty fibers, so don't attempt it! I use my iron sparingly on this type of fabric, usually only on seams or other places where it may need to be tamed a bit. Because it is a synthetic fabric, it won't wrinkle, so ironing is a minimal requirement anyway.

How should fleece be cut? I have used regular scissors, a rotary cutter and even pinking shears on the fabric and they all work well. The pinking shears are only for decorative purposes since the fabric does not fray. If I need to cut a long piece fairly straight, I prefer a rotary cutter.

Now that you know some basics of handling this fabric, let your only limit be your imagination!

Fleece comes in many weights and can be used for all types of projects. Its durability and weather resistance makes it great for neckwear and headbands as well as outerwear.

Sewing Advice
Making Fabric Flowers

I love to make flowers from fabric! I have made them with just about every kind of fabric around—cottons, velvet, twill, silk, wool, felt, fleece—the list goes on and on. The process for making fabric flowers is very simple, yet the results look like they took a lot of time to achieve. Soon, you will be thinking of all the items you can add the flourish of a flower to!

To get started, think narrow. I like for flowers to be compact rather than floppy, as I think they look more natural this way. This means that the strips cut for flowers will be narrow. Since fabrics like cotton, twill, silk and velvet tend to fray, I cut the strips from these fabrics twice as wide as what I will need, then fold them in half so that the raw edges are along the bottom. Because fraying isn't a concern with wool, felt or fleece, I cut the width exactly how I want it when the flower is finished.

The flowers that you will be making here most resemble a rose or other full bloom type of blossom.

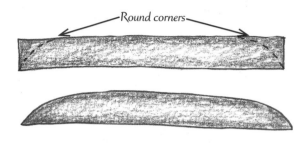

Round corners

1   Cut the strips of fabric to make the flowers. For fabrics that fray, cut a 2" (or narrower) strip. After you have made a few flowers, you will know what you like best. Remember that this strip will be folded in half widthwise, wrong sides together, before the flower is made.

For nonfraying fabrics, cut the width of the strip 1¼" or narrower. Just cut the full width of fabric as this will be cut down in the next few steps.

2   For fraying fabrics, gather your strip on the machine. This is easy and fast if you have a ruffler attachment. I set mine to gather at every 6th stitch or at every stitch if I want a tighter bloom. If you do not have a ruffler attachment, complete a line of long straight stitches near the raw edge down the length of the strip, then pull the bobbin thread to gather it up. Once the gathering has been completed, press the gathering flat.

For nonfraying fabrics, predetermine the length of the strip, then gather by hand with a long running stitch. For a larger flower, go with about 12" in length. For a smaller flower, go with a 6" length. Once the length has been cut, round the top edges.

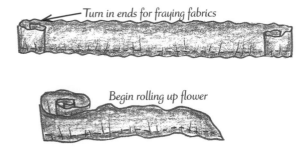

Turn in ends for fraying fabrics

Begin rolling up flower

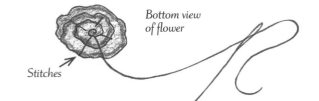

Bottom view of flower

Stitches

3 Once the strip has been gathered, begin rolling up the gathered strip. For fraying fabrics, I usually turn under the beginning and ending edges to conceal the raw edge. Because these types of fabrics are thinner than fleece or wool, it will take a much longer length to make a full bloom. You may even find that you need the entire width of the fabric for one flower. Again, this is based on your personal preference.

4 As the strip is being rolled, have a hand needle that is threaded with a sturdy polyester thread. I usually double the thread for extra strength. Begin taking stitches through the layers along the rolled edge to hold the flower together.

5 Continue rolling and stitching until the flower is sewn together. Take a few stitches to secure the bottom edge of the flower, then cut the thread. To add the flower to a project, pin it in place, then hand-stitch to secure.

Winter Sewing Project

Fleecy Rose Scarf

FABRICS

⅓ yd. polar fleece or ⅙ yd. each of two colors

⅛ yd. contrasting color for the roses

NOTIONS

1 yd. of ¼" wide elastic

Fabric marking pencil, such as Sewline

Polyester thread to match fabrics

Rotary cutter, ruler and mat

Large safety pin

This simple-to-sew scarf keeps you super warm while looking stylish, all at the same time. The construction is so easy that you will find reasons to make more than one! This project makes a fast and thoughtful gift for a special friend or family member. Because the scarf is composed of two layers of fleece, you could easily get a totally different look by using two coordinating or contrasting colors. The addition of elastic down the center with a hidden opening to pull the end through makes the scarf slightly springy in nature and adds to the comfort level. The roses are optional, so if an unadorned look is more your style, simply leave them off.

Keep it Clean

When working with polar fleece, you may get a bit of fuzzy lint floating around in your sewing space. I like to keep a sticky lint roller handy to pick up the lint as I cut, keeping any messes to a minimum.

The finished scarf is 38" long x 6" wide.

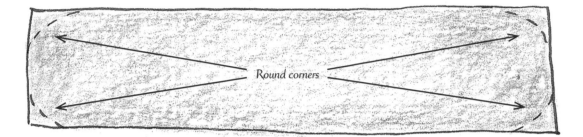

Round corners

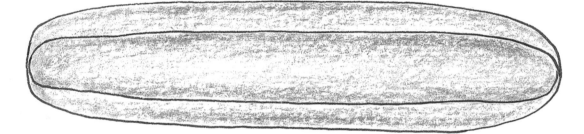

- - - · CUT AND STITCH THE SCARF · - - -

1   Cut two strips from your fabric, one 6 " wide and one 4 " wide.

2   Trim the selvedges from the narrow ends.

3   Slightly round the corners of each strip.

4   Layer the narrow strip on top of the wider one, centered with ends even. Pin together.

5   Use a seam guide on your machine set at 2¾ " from the needle if you have one. If you do not, measure out to the right of the needle by 2¾ " and place a piece of masking tape or sticky note as your guide.

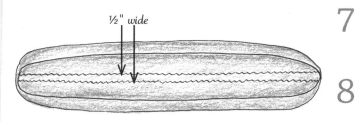

½" wide

6   Set the machine for a long, narrow zigzag stitch. I set mine at a width of 2.8 and length of 1.1.

7   Stitch the layers together with the wider edge against the seam guide. Turn and stitch down the other side. This will create a ½" casing down the center of the scarf.

8   To make the opening to pull one end of the scarf through, measure 6" up from one end and mark to one side of the casing stitching. Mark again at 9" from the end.

9   Starting at one mark, stitch down the length between the two marks. Pivot and stitch, only about 2 stitches in length. Pivot again and stitch down the other side, then across the other end. This creates the opening. Snip carefully with scissors, then cut open to the ends.

6"

9"

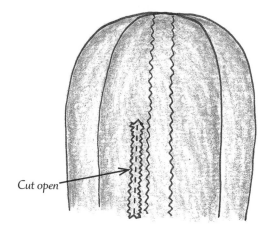

Cut open

Narrow layer together

Stitch this line to hold narrow layers together

Wide layer together

Stitching from elastic casing

--- --- INSERT THE ELASTIC --- --- -

1 Place the large safety pin into the end of the elastic and pull it through the casing. Watch the elastic end carefully and when it is just inside the casing, stitch across the end, ½" in from the edge of the fabric. Stitch across a few times to secure, then continue pulling the elastic through the casing. Once the elastic has been pulled all the way through, remove the safety pin and allow the end of the elastic to slip just inside the casing. Stitch across the end to secure.

--- --- FINISH THE RUFFLES --- --- -

1 Distribute the gathering evenly along the length of the scarf. To give it some dimension, open out the layers so that the narrow layer is folded in half widthwise with the casing in between.

2 Keeping the wider layer folded out of the way, stitch down the length of the narrow sections to stitch them together over the casing, stopping when you reach the opening. Start again after the opening and continue down the rest of the length of the scarf.

--- --- MAKE AND ATTACH THE ROSES --- -

1 Make a series of fleece roses to nest inside the ruffles. There are a total of 13 roses pictured, 6 large and 7 small. For the large roses, cut six 12" × 1¼" strips. For the small roses, cut seven 6" × 1" strips. Follow the instructions on page 102 to make the roses.

2 Once the roses are complete, try on the scarf by placing it around your neck and pulling the end through the opening on the other end. Adjust as you want to wear it, then begin pinning the roses in groups around the length of the scarf, nesting them in and around the ruffles.

3 Stitch the roses in place.

" Time for Reflection

How do you feel about working with fleece? Will you use it for other projects? And if so, what ideas are brewing?

_____
_____
_____
_____
_____
_____
_____
_____

What color combinations did you use for your scarf? What would you like to try?

_____
_____
_____
_____
_____
_____
_____
_____
_____
_____

What other ideas do you have for making the scarf different?

_____
_____
_____
_____
_____
_____
_____

"

Sewing Advice
Working With Different Closures

There are so many great types of closures for projects that it is sometimes hard to decide on one! When trying to make a decision, it is important to think about how the project will be used. Is it important to be able to have quick access, or is the aesthetic nature more important? For me, it is usually both!

Here are some great closures to consider along with their advantages:

⬦ **Magnetic Snaps:** Magnetic snaps come in a variety of sizes, shapes and finishes. They are often used for bag closure. They pull apart and snap together easily. Most have a set of prongs and a reinforcement plate for the installation. They are easy to add with a pair of small pliers. Remember that magnetic snaps must be added before a lining so that the prong portion is nicely concealed.

⬦ **Twist Locks:** A twist lock is a nice alternative to a magnetic snap, especially on bags with flap closures. Access to the contents of the bag will not be quite as quick, but you do get the added aesthetic quality of the hardware, which can be a nice finish. Most twist locks have a prong installation that is similar to a magnetic snap. In order to conceal the prongs, the twisting or center portion is installed in the same manner as a magnetic snap, which means you'll want to attach it before adding the lining. The outside or plate of the lock requires you to cut a hole in the flap or whatever you are adding it to. Doing so ensures that both sides of the plate are seen. Attach the outside plate after the piece you will be adding it to is complete.

⬦ **Hook and Loop Tape:** This type of closure is best when it's important to hold items in place or when other types of hardware aren't aesthetically desired. For example, if you want the focus to be centered more around the design of the fabric or the project itself, you may opt to use hook and loop tape in place of adding flashy hardware. Hook and loop tape provides the most secure closure (next to a zipper, of course) to keep items from falling out of a bag or pocket. As such, they work great for insulated bags. What's more, you can purchase these closures at most craft or fabric stores. If you decide to use hook and loop tape for a project, I recommend the sew-in type. I would also advise that you refrain from sewing through the self-adhesive type, as this could damage your machine!

⬦ **Zippers:** Zippers make wonderful closures. There are many different types of zippers available, and your choice will depend on what you are making. My favorite zipper to use in bags is the sport zipper. It has a more substantial appearance and holds up well to a lot of use. Most zippers come in a myriad of colors, making them suitable for just about any project. The installation is a bit more involved than with other types of closures, but the finished result is well worth it. Once you have mastered the zipper, you will think of countless projects to add them to!

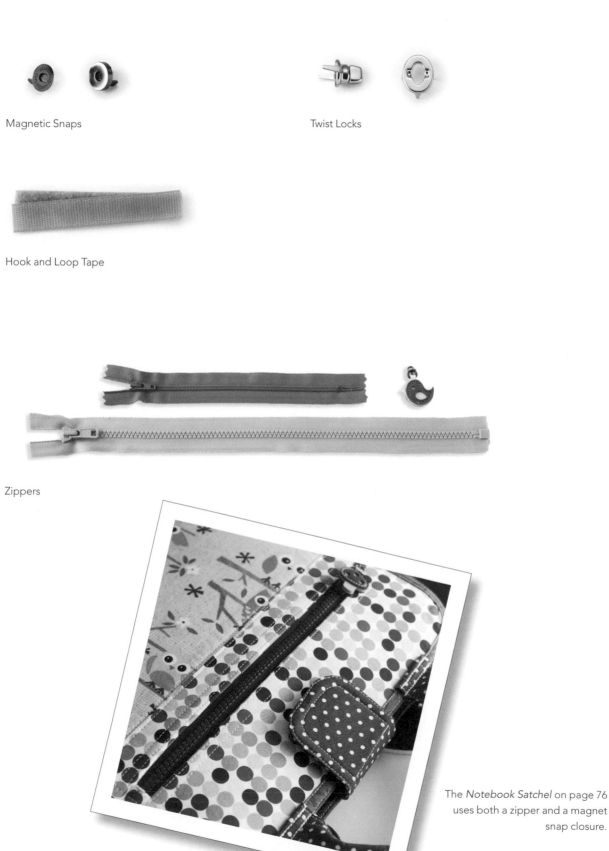

Magnetic Snaps

Twist Locks

Hook and Loop Tape

Zippers

The *Notebook Satchel* on page 76 uses both a zipper and a magnet snap closure.

Sewing Advice
Taking Care of Machine Maintenance

I don't know about you, but my machines really take a lot of abuse when I am hard at work. It is important to remember to stop every once in a while (more often than not) and check on a few things to be sure that your equipment is in good working order. A little preventative maintenance can go a long way towards keeping your machine out of the shop!

Here are some things to remember:

- **Keep your machine clean.** After many hours of sewing, lint becomes trapped in the machine, especially around the feed dogs and in the bobbin area. It is a good idea to take these areas apart and blow or brush out the lint. Watch the area around the needle as well to avoid lint or dust clogs. It's also a good idea to wipe down the outside of the machine periodically to keep dust and lint at bay.

- **Keep your machine oiled.** Purchase some good quality machine oil and place a few drops in the bobbin area with the bobbin removed. Run the motor of the machine for about 30 seconds to allow the lubrication to distribute through the parts. Do this with all of the thread removed from the machine.

- **Keep your needle sharp.** After continued sewing, a needle becomes dull. This can lead to thread breakage, skipped stitches or snagged fabric. Even if the needle looks okay after repeated use, it can still be dull. Thus, to avoid damaging your projects, be sure to change needles fairly regularly.

- **Watch your machine feet.** Check the integrity of your machine feet often and replace any damaged pieces. This will improve your sewing experience and is best for the life of the machine as well.

- **Use good quality thread.** This may seem like a minor thing, but using the best quality of thread you can afford will be easier for the machine (less lint), and the stitches will actually look better!

- **Keep your machine serviced.** Make it a goal to get your machine serviced once a year, no matter how much or how little you sew. This goes a long way to preventing trouble when you least need it, like in the middle of the night when you are trying to finish something! I recommend keeping a service log next to your workspace as a reminder to have your machine annually serviced. (See pages 122–123 for a sample service log.)

- **Aim to keep your machine clean and oil it often**. When I am doing heavy sewing (this translates to several hours a day for days at a time), I clean my machine once a week and oil it about every two weeks. If you are sewing less, then you will not need to clean and oil as often. As a general rule, check your machine before you sew. Your machine will thank you for it!

Sewing Advice
Staying Organized: A Notion for Your Notions

Sewing requires you to have a lot of different notions. The more experienced and adventurous you become, the more supplies you seem to accumulate. After a while, this can become an organizational nightmare, but it doesn't have to!

I have found using plastic bins with tight-fitting lids to be my salvation. I label the ends, listing the contents of the bins (e.g., buttons, zippers, bag hardware, etc.). I stack the bins inside my studio closet or island. When I get ready to use my supplies, I know exactly where to find everything, which means no wasted time digging around for what I need. A nice set of shelves on your studio walls work well, too. Likewise, you can use large decorative jars instead of bins, which adds visual interest to your room to boot!

Another great tip for staying organized is that while it's okay to stay well stocked on the essentials, also keep in mind that you don't have to have every thread color ever made. I find that I use neutral colors more than anything else. After you have a bit of sewing experience, you will be amazed at how well a neutral thread will blend with the fabric. The colors I like to keep on hand at all times are white, cream, tan, light gray, black and brown. You can throw navy blue in there, too, if you tend to sew with blues. This goes for zippers as well.

When it comes to shopping, it's important to remember that you don't need to make a run to the store for an essential notion at the start of every new project. Instead, keep your eye out for good sales. This is a perfect time to stock up on your most used notions, ensuring they'll be close at hand when they are most needed.

My final tip for staying organized is to keep mulitples of certain essentials. For instance, I keep a pair of scissors at the ironing board, my cutting area and the sewing machine table. I also do this with straight pins/pin cushions, marking pencils, adjustable rulers and point turners. That way, when I'm hard at work, I have all the necessary tools no matter where I happen to be.

Winter Sewing Project

Embellished Earwarmer

FABRICS

⅛ yd. wool

⅛ yd. polar fleece

NOTIONS

1½" piece of ¾" wide hook and loop tape

Approximately 17 large beads

Flexible measuring tape

Freezer paper for the pattern templates

Hand embroidery needle

Pearl 5 cotton embroidery thread in desired color (project featured uses 844)

Pinking shears

Polyester thread to match fabrics

This simple yet stylish earwarmer consists mostly of handwork. And, since all you'll need most of the time is a needle and thread, it also travels easily! Don't you just love projects you can take on the go with you?

The perfect combination of fleece and wool, this project is ideal for winter. With the warm, soft fleece layer closest to your skin, it is sure to keep your ears warm on those cold windy days. Not to mention, it's pretty cute to boot!

The flower is a little different as it is made from 6 heart-shaped pieces. I love that it stands away from the project, lending a nice dimensional quality. The hand embroidery work is completed with Pearl 5 cotton in backstitch.

I think this earwarmer would be equally pretty in cream wool with a black layer of fleece behind it. The flower could be made in red wool with dark brown branches and a few red beads for the berries—very wintery and lovely, indeed!

Upcycling Materials for Your Projects

If you're feeling green—environmentally friendly, that is —upcycling old materials is the way to go. You could always re-purpose an old wool sweater or scarf that you no longer use to make this earwarmer. Just wash it in hot water to felt it, then cut it to make the background for your embroidery!

The finished earwarmer is 3" wide at the widest point, tapering to 1½" at the ends, with a total overall length of 24". The overlap is 2". This is designed for a 22" circumference. If your head is smaller or larger, the pattern piece can be altered to fit.

1 Using a measuring tape, measure around your head at the base of your skull, going around your ears to the upper part of your forehead. Take note of the measurement. Remember that this earwarmer pattern is designed for a head measurement of 22" with a 2" overlap. If you measure larger than that, do as follows:

✧ If you measure 23", add ½" on the fold of the pattern. This will add 1 full inch.

✧ If you measure 24", add 1" on the fold of the pattern. This will add 2 full inches.

MAKE THE PATTERN AND CUT OUT FABRIC

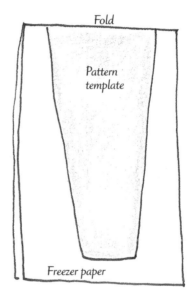

1 Trace the patterns onto a folded piece of freezer paper and cut out, making any necessary alterations to the pattern on the folded portion. Cut out and then open out the paper so that you have a full pattern.

2 Lay the freezer paper template shiny-side down on the fleece and very lightly iron it to stick the template temporarily. Cut out fabric, then peel away the template. Repeat for the wool piece.

3 Using the pinking shears, trim about ⅛" from each edge of the wool piece to make it slightly smaller than the fleece piece. After trimming, lay it on top of the fleece and do any extra trimming as necessary. It is important for the fleece to just show slightly around all the edges.

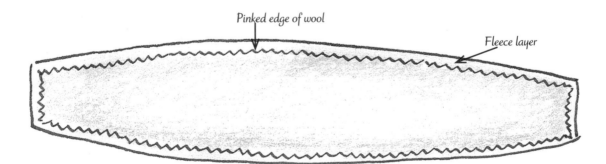

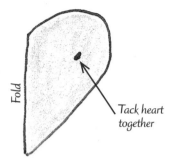

Fold

Tack heart together

Whipstitched edges

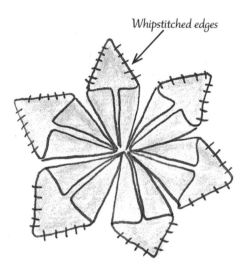

- - - - - - - MAKE THE FLOWER - - - - - -

1   Cut 6 hearts from the wool fabric using the freezer paper template.

2   Fold each heart down the center and tack the upper rounded parts together as shown.

3   Double thread a hand needle and join all 6 hearts together through the top as shown:

4   Pull the thread tight and take a few stitches to secure.

5   Add a large bead to the center of the flower.

6   Place the flower to one side of the center and whipstitch the edges in place using the Pearl 5 cotton.

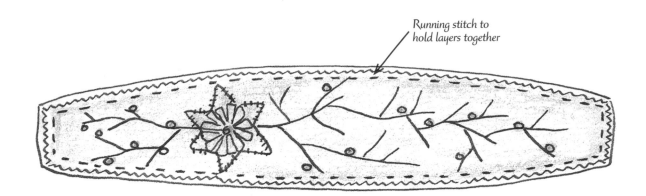

Running stitch to hold layers together

EMBROIDER THE WOOL AND ADD BEADS

1 Backstitch the branches for the berries to either side of the flower. I freeformed this stitching, starting with a line and then branching off of it. If you do not feel comfortable freeform stitching, draw a few lines to follow with a fabric marking pencil.

2 Add large beads throughout the backstitching.

3 Press the embroidery work from the wrong side, then add the wool portion to the fleece section, making sure that the fleece is visible on all edges. Pin the layers together.

4 Secure the two layers together with a running stitch and Pearl 5 cotton.

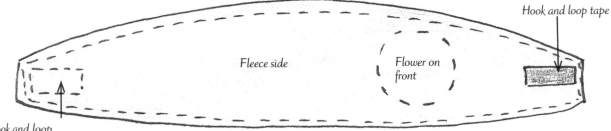

Hook and loop tape

Fleece side

Flower on front

Hook and loop tape on other side

ADD THE CLOSURE

1 Place the hook side of the hook and loop tape on the wool portion near one end. Stitch in place. Place the loop side of the hook and loop tape on the fleece portion of the other end and stitch in place.

Time for Reflection

What did you like about working with wool?

_____
_____
_____
_____
_____
_____
_____
_____

What do you think about pearl cotton as compared with regular embroidery floss? Which do you prefer and why?

_____
_____
_____
_____
_____
_____
_____
_____
_____

If you wanted to do more of this project on the machine, how would you accomplish that?

_____
_____
_____
_____
_____
_____
_____

NOTES

NOTES

Machine Service Log

Shop name: _____

Shop address: _____

Website: _____

Phone: _____ E-mail: _____

My mechanic's name: _____

Other notes: _____

_____

_____

Last serviced on: _____

Drop off: _____ Pick up: _____

Cost: _____

Service included: _____

_____

_____

_____

_____

Last serviced on: _____

Drop off: _____ Pick up: _____

Cost: _____

Service included: _____

_____

_____

_____

_____

Last serviced on: _____

Drop off: _____ Pick up: _____

Cost: _____

Service included: _____

_____

_____

_____

_____

Last serviced on: _____

Drop off: _____ Pick up: _____

Cost: _____

Service included: _____

_____

_____

_____

_____

Machine Service Log

Shop name: _____

Shop address: _____

Website: _____

Phone: _____ E-mail: _____

My mechanic's name: _____

Other notes: _____

_____

_____

Last serviced on:_____

Drop off: _____ Pick up: _____

Cost: _____

Service included: _____

_____

_____

_____

_____

Last serviced on:_____

Drop off: _____ Pick up: _____

Cost: _____

Service included: _____

_____

_____

_____

_____

Last serviced on: _____

Drop off: _____ Pick up: _____

Cost: _____

Service included: _____

_____

_____

_____

_____

Last serviced on:_____

Drop off: _____ Pick up: _____

Cost: _____

Service included: _____

_____

_____

_____

_____

Resources

FABRIC

Wholesale to the trade only

Michael Miller Fabrics
118 West 22nd Street, 5th Floor
New York, NY 10011
www.michaelmillerfabrics.com

Moda Fabrics
13800 Hutton Drive
Dallas, TX 75234
www.unitednotions.com

Riley Blake
375 South Main Street
Alpine, Utah 84004
www.rileyblakedesigns.com

STABILIZERS

Pellon
150 2nd Avenue
St. Petersburg, FL 33701
www.pellonideas.com

BAG HARDWARE

The Buckle Guy
www.buckleguy.com

Strapworks
3900 West 1st Avenue
Eugene, OR 97402
www.strapworks.com

Jo-Ann Fabric & Craft Stores
5555 Darrow Road
Hudson, OH 44236
www.joann.com

Purse Supply Depot
10661 Fulton Court
Rancho Cucamonga, CA 91730
www.pursesupplydepot.com

Dritz Notions
Prym Consumer USA Inc.
P.O. Box 5028
Spartanburg, SC 29304
www.dritz.com

LIGHTING

OttLite
220 West 7th Avenue, Suite 100
Tampa, FL 33602
www.ottlite.com

IRONS & IRONING PRODUCTS

Rowenta
20 Constitution Blvd. South
Shelton CT 06484
www.shoprowenta.com

SCISSORS

Gingher
130 Kentucky Street
Petaluma, CA 94952
www.gingher.us

CUTTING TOOLS & ROTARY MATS

Olfa
5500 N. Pearl Street, Suite 400
Rosemont, IL 60018
www.olfa.com

MEASURING TOOLS

Omnigrid
Prym Consumer USA Inc.
P.O. Box 5028
Spartanburg, SC 29304
www.dritz.com

EMBROIDERY FLOSS

DMC
10 Basin Drive, Suite 130
Kearny, NJ 07032
www.dmc-usa.com

Index

www.fwmedia.com

16 15 14 13 12   5 4 3 2 1

DISTRIBUTED IN CANADA BY FRASER DIRECT
100 Armstrong Avenue
Georgetown, ON, Canada L7G 5S4
Tel: (905) 877-4411

DISTRIBUTED IN THE U.K. AND EUROPE BY F&W MEDIA INTERNATIONAL
Brunel House, Newton Abbot, Devon, TQ12 4PU, England
Tel: (+44) 1626 323200, Fax: (+44) 1626 323319
Email: enquiries@fwmedia.com

DISTRIBUTED IN AUSTRALIA BY CAPRICORN LINK
P.O. Box 704, S. Windsor NSW, 2756 Australia
Tel: (02) 4577-3555

SRN: V7974
ISBN-13: 978-1-4402-3198-8

Editor: Layne Vanover
Desk Editor: Noel Rivera
Designer: Charly Bailey
Production Coordinator: Greg Nock
Illustrator: Kay Whitt
Photographer: Lorna Yabsley

Metric Conversion Chart		
To convert	**to**	**multiply by**
Inches	Centimeters	2.54
Centimeters	Inches	0.4
Feet	Centimeters	30.5
Centimeters	Feet	0.03
Yards	Meters	0.9
Meters	Yards	1.1

About the author

"Love what you do, and you will never work a day in your life."

In a nutshell, this quote describes exactly the way Kay Whitt feels about her work as a pattern designer for clothing and accessories. After spending nine years as an elementary school teacher (sewing in her spare time), she resigned from teaching and launched her pattern company. Since then, Kay has earned a reputation for her innovative designs and clear instructions, making her patterns some of the most popular in the marketplace, and written the bestselling *Sew Serendipity* and *Sew Serendipity Bags*.

Kay resides in Texas with her husband, Keith, and their bird, ET. She is always busy working on something new and exciting and never tires of sharing her passion for design and sewing. See what Kay is up to at blog.sewserendipity.com.